# LAMP OF WISDOM

This book is a restricted text intended for students who have completed a Rigdzin introductory retreat. Please do not distribute or share this book. Exposure to some of these ideas before a direct introduction in meditation can harden the mind with conceptualization and make the realizations more difficult to recognize. Please protect these precious teachings so that others can benefit directly.

Lamp of Wisdom: A Modern Guide to the Gradual Path of Enlightenment

ISBN: 978-0-9892289-1-6

Published by Bright Alliance

First Edition

Printed and Bound in the United States of America

Layout and design by Brad Reynolds www.integralartandstudies.com

# LAMP OF WISDOM

## A Modern Guide to
## the Gradual Path of Enlightenment

### DUSTIN DIPERNA
RIGDZIN KHYENTSE ÖZER

This book is structured as a gradual path to enlightenment. It balances traditional Buddhist wisdom with modern psychological insights. It begins with foundational teachings and systematically unfolds into the highest realizations of Mahamudra and Dzogchen, culminating in the realization that Enlightened Awareness is both universal and uniquely expressed in each being.

## Dedication

To my spiritual mentor, Daniel P. Brown, a true master of the pointing out style of teaching. And to all the great lineage masters who keep the teachings fresh and alive in their mindstream. May this book bring endless benefit to all beings.

# TABLE OF CONTENTS

# LAMP OF WISDOM

*A Modern Guide to
the Gradual Path of Enlightenment*

# Chapter 1

# A LAMP OF WISDOM IN THE MODERN WORLD

## Why Awakening Still Matters Today

In every era, humanity has sought answers to the same fundamental questions: What is the meaning of life? How do we find lasting fulfillment? What is our true nature? These questions have guided countless seekers, philosophers, and mystics throughout history. The Buddhist path, particularly the Lamrim or "Gradual Path to Awakening," offers a systematic, time-tested approach to these inquiries, guiding individuals from confusion to wisdom, from suffering to liberation.

In this book, I invite you to journey through this gradual path as a living practice that is both profoundly ancient and strikingly relevant to the modern world. *A Lamp of Wisdom*[1] serves as both a map and a companion, illuminating a path that countless practitioners have walked before.

By following a clear and integrated framework, you can wake up to your true nature, heal the wounds that keep you fragmented and grow into a fully embodied, compassionate being who brings wisdom into the world.

---

1. The title of this book is inspired by the text: "A Lamp of Wisdom" (Prajñāpradīpa) – by Bhāvaviveka (c. 500–578): A crucial commentary on Nāgārjuna's Madhyamaka philosophy, clarifying the nature of emptiness and refuting opposing views.

### Why This Book? Why Now?

There is already a rich history of treatises that articulate a stage-based approach to enlightenment. Texts such as Atisha's Lamp for the Path to Enlightenment and Tsongkhapa's Great Treatise on the Stages of the Path present the whole Buddhist path as a gradual progression. These texts remain foundational and invaluable. At the same time, there is tremendous benefit in updating classic teachings to resonate with the evolving contours of our modern world.

The world we live in today is very different from that of traditional Tibet or India. Most of us are not monks or nuns. Many of us don't live within a supportive cultural or social structure that allows for years of study or long-term retreat committed to traditional Buddhist practice. Some of you reading this book might not even identify as a Buddhist in the first place!

Today, we live in a complex, fast-paced environment shaped by psychological insights, neuroscience, trauma research, and global interconnectedness. We need a way to practice a path to enlightenment that is faithful to the essence of Buddhism while still remaining relevant and accessible in modern life.

This book is an attempt to do just that. In the following chapters, I try to balance preservation and innovation. My intention is to honor the timeless wisdom of the traditional gradual path, while weaving in modern scientific insight, psychological depth, and a style of teaching that speaks to the needs of our time.

### Why I'm Writing This:
### My Journey on the Path

To understand why I'm writing this book, I want to share a bit about my own journey. I did not come to Buddhism through blind faith or cultural inheritance. My approach has always been one of rigorous inquiry, deep practice, and a desire to integrate the best of Eastern wisdom and Western knowledge.

In my family of origin, we didn't practice a specific religious tradition but there was always an attitude of open-mindedness and exploration. When I was young, my mother used to hint at the possibility that there was something more to life than what appeared. She'd speak about God as the universe and that the universe is love. In this way, she planted the seeds of Awakening in my heart. My father was an exemplar of generosity, diligence, and the entrepreneurial spirit. He would always tell me how important it was to "work hard" and to "learn how to learn." He planted the seeds in me of how to show up with care, impact, and power. I took the advice of both of my parents to heart and it has guided my life.

After graduating from Cornell University, I spent my twenties working closely with American philosopher Ken Wilber. Ken Wilber was my first true mentor outside of my parents. I could go to him with any issue and could share everything with him. I talked to him about my romantic ordeals, my ever-deepening philosophical ideas about life, and my most profound questions about Awakening. Each time I came to him, he would respond with love and attunement, and he would always broaden and deepen my view.

Ken Wilber, often referred to as the "Einstein of Consciousness research," is the originator of Integral Theory. Integral Theory is a comprehensive model of psycho-social development that weaves together ancient wisdom and modern psychology along with a complex understanding of language, history, and social and cultural transformation. Because of its depth and breadth, Integral Theory is sometimes called "A Theory of Everything." My exposure to Integral Theory at a young age gave me a broad intellectual foundation that I con-

3

tinue to use for all the work I do now. More than 20 years into our relationship, Ken and I remain in very close contact and share a deep friendship.

After a powerful and immersive time with Ken Wilber, I attended graduate school at Harvard University to study our world's great religious traditions. While in graduate school, I worked closely under the guidance of a Harvard professor and renowned Western meditation master, Daniel P. Brown. Dan Brown served as both my graduate thesis advisor and as my primary meditation teacher. After a few years of working together academically and learning from him as his meditation student, Dan Brown invited me to join him even more intimately as an apprentice in learning to teach meditation. Under his wing and careful supervision, I learned how to guide others in Mahamudra and Dzogchen meditation. Overall, I studied with Dan for 16 years. We spent many of those years teaching together, side by side. Our embodied relationship lasted until he passed away in 2022. I am forever grateful for the kindness he showed me and the exquisite training he gave me. He is always with me.

Over the years, I have also worked closely with other teachers and therapists in modern psychology, trauma healing, and positive psychology. These relationships have helped me see that spiritual Awakening alone does not always resolve deep-seated emotional wounds. Many practitioners over-intellectualize spirituality, using it to bypass unresolved trauma rather than fully integrating it into their growth. I've seen this pattern play out not just in others but in myself as well. Decades of personal work, healing, and integration have given me firsthand experience of the amazing systems of therapeutic intervention we now have at our fingertips.

Lastly, for the past seven years, I've held a teaching appointment at Stanford University and the role of Co-Editor-in-Chief at the mental health company CredibleMind.

These positions keep me up to date with all of the latest academic research in these areas. Through teaching, writing, and leadership in the fields of meditation and human flourishing, I've had the privilege of guiding thousands of students along this path. Through all of my experience, I've learned what truly works to move from conceptual understanding to lived Awakening.

In its most authentic expression, the transmission of realization is an unbroken string of pearls threaded together with love. If I share anything of value in this book, it is only the result of the incredible wisdom and love I've received from my own teachers and mentors. One of the main ways I express my gratitude to them is by keeping their wisdom and realization alive by passing it on to you. Everything I offer here is shared with the deep wish that it brings benefit to you. May the essence of this transmission lineage plant the seeds in your heart of everything good.

## Four Dimensions of Spiritual Wholeness

Over the years, Ken Wilber and I worked together to articulate four core dimensions of spiritual wholeness. These dimensions are essential for a fully embodied, integrated path of Awakening. They are: *Wake Up, Grow Up, Clean Up, Show Up*.

**Wake Up** – Waking up refers to the direct experience of our deepest nature. It reveals a vast nondual ocean of love at the core of our very being. Through meditation, we cultivate stability (*shamatha*) and insight (*vipaśyanā*), eventually seeing through the illusion of a separate self and separate world. Mahamudra and Dzogchen offer direct pathways to this recognition of unbounded wholeness.

**Grow Up** – Awakening alone is not enough. We must mature psychologically and integrate stages of development that allow for emotional intelligence, healthy relationships, and ethical conduct.

**Clean Up** – Many people seek spiritual realization while ignoring unresolved trauma, emotional wounds, and subconscious conditioning. True freedom requires deep healing and integration of the relative self. This is relative wholeness.

**Show Up** – The fruit of the path is not escape, but an engaged, active presence in the world. True realization expresses itself in service, compassion, and action for the benefit of all beings.

These four dimensions are the heart essence of Integral Theory. And although this book emphasizes "waking up," Awakening is best held in the larger context of these other core dimensions of spiritual wholeness. I touch on each of these dimensions throughout this book.[2]

## The Path Begins Here

In the chapters ahead, we will explore the timeless wisdom of Buddhism through a contemporary integral lens, honoring the depth of tradition while making it fully accessible for today's practitioners.

This book is not meant to convince you of anything. It is an invitation: a lamp to illuminate your own direct experience. The path is here, waiting. The question is:

Are you ready to deepen the journey?

---

2. I've written elsewhere quite extensively about these areas and I encourage interested readers to see my other books for further detail. In particular, the reader is encouraged to read my book *Streams of Wisdom*.

# Chapter 2

# THE GRADUAL PATH TO ENLIGHTENMENT

## Why We Need a Step-by-Step Approach to Liberation

We live in an age of instant gratification. From the moment we get out of bed, we are bombarded with notifications, fast-moving headlines, and promises of quick solutions to life's deepest struggles. Whether it's biohacking for peak performance, therapy techniques for immediate relief, or even spiritual Awakening in seven easy steps, our culture is obsessed with the idea that transformation should be fast, effortless, and guaranteed.

But for most of us, complete enlightenment, which fully liberates us from egoic suffering and causes the flourishing of everything good, does not happen overnight. Even in traditions that emphasize sudden Awakening, after realization has occurred, this realization must be stabilized, integrated, and embodied over time. So although the initial Awakening to your true nature happens in a single instant, the gradual path to Enlightenment emphasizes how to nurture that Awakening to its full fruition.

This is why the gradual path exists. It is a graceful unfolding, guiding us step by step from confusion to clarity, from suffering to wisdom, from self-centeredness to compassionate presence.

## The Three Types of Students: Instantaneous, Leaping, Gradual

In the Buddhist tradition, practitioners are often categorized into three types of students based on how they progress toward realization. The three categories are: (1) the instantaneous type, (2) those who leap, and (3) those who progress gradually. Each path reflects a different way of Awakening, yet all ultimately lead to the same realization.

The instantaneous type of student is the rarest. This is the type of student who, upon hearing a single teaching or encountering the right conditions, directly realizes the nature of mind. Their karma and past practice have ripened to a point where no further preparation is needed. They awaken in a single moment. The instantaneous student is like a dry twig bursting into flame with the slightest spark. While this is often idealized, it is not the common experience for most practitioners.

The leaping type of student progresses in great strides. They move through long periods with little progress followed by sudden breakthroughs. These practitioners may feel like growth is slow, only to have profound insights that propel them forward, often skipping stages along the way. Their path is marked by alternating phases of plateau and leaping ahead.

Most of us, however, are *gradual students*. Awakening unfolds step by step, like water slowly wearing down a stone. Through consistent practice and by cultivating ethical conduct, meditation, and wisdom, we refine our perception and clear away obscurations over time. For gradual practitioners, the path requires patience, steady effort, and trust in the process. While the journey may not be full of fireworks, it builds an unshakable foundation for lasting realization. Recognizing ourselves as gradual students allows us to embrace the practice with humility and dedication, knowing that every moment of effort is shaping our Awakening.

This book is written for the gradual type of student.

## The Need for a Roadmap

Imagine you want to climb Mount Everest. You wouldn't simply fly to Nepal, put on some hiking boots, and start walking toward the summit. You would need to train, prepare, and acclimate to the altitude before even beginning the ascent. In addition to this, you'd want to have a good map and a trusted guide to show you the way.

Spiritual practice is no different. The mind is conditioned by years, perhaps lifetimes, of habitual patterns, distortions, and false identifications. Simply reading about Awakening or having one profound meditation experience is not enough. Without a clear roadmap, we can get lost, discouraged, or misled by experiences that seem profound but do not actually lead to lasting enlightenment.

The Lamrim, or "Stages of the Path," provides a roadmap to show us the way. It systematically clarifies what is essential, showing us where we are and what we need to cultivate next. It is a proven approach that has led countless practitioners to liberation, not just monks and nuns, but householders, leaders, and everyday people like us.

## The Key Stages of the Gradual Path

This book is structured according to a modern Lamrim, incorporating both classical Buddhist wisdom and contemporary psychological insights. Each chapter covers a critical aspect in the Awakening process, moving from foundational teachings to the most profound realizations of Enlightened Awareness. Here is the progression I've laid out in this book:

1. **The Precious Opportunity of Human Life— Recognizing the Rarity of This Life** – Human birth is rare and offers a unique chance for Awakening, emphasizing the importance of living with intention.

2. **Impermanence and The Reality of Death— Embracing Change as the Heart of the Path** – Recognizing the transient nature of existence liberates us from fear and attachment, allowing us to engage spiritual practice with urgency and full presence.

3. **Karma and the Power of Cause and Effect— Shaping Our Destiny Through Intentional Action** – Our thoughts, words, and actions shape our experience, and by transforming negative karma and planting positive seeds, we create positive future conditions for Awakening.

4. **Understanding Suffering—The Cause of Suffering and Its End** – By understanding the nature of dukkha (suffering) and its causes, we learn to transform suffering into wisdom and liberation.

5. **Finding True Refuge—Resting in What is Unshakable** – True refuge lies in coming to know our deepest nature through the Buddha, Dharma, and Sangha, rather than in fleeting external sources such as materialism, status, or relationships.

6. **Living an Ethical Life—Growing Up and Showing Up** – Ethical conduct, practiced through restraint, cultivation of virtue, and wisdom-based action, forms the basis of inner peace and deepens our spiritual path.

7. **The Four Immeasurables—The Boundless Qualities of an Awakened Heart** – By cultivating equanimity, unconditional love, compassion,

and sympathetic joy, we train the heart to expand beyond self-centered care.

8. **Bodhicitta—Awakening for the Benefit of All Beings** – The shift from personal liberation to universal Awakening arises through relative and ultimate bodhicitta. Thus transforms into the wish that both you and all beings find total and complete enlightenment.

9. **The Six Perfections—Bringing Wisdom and Compassion into Action** – Generosity, ethics, patience, joyful effort, concentration, and wisdom serve as the living expression of bodhicitta, integrating awakened activity into everyday life.

10. **Concentration Meditation—Taming the Mind** – There are nine stages of concentration to calm and stabilize the mind. When the mind is properly trained, we can turn the mind to examine our own direct experience, leading to insight.

11. **Insight Meditation—Seeing Through Relative Experience** – Through the Three Turnings of the Wheel, we move beyond fixed identity, seeing impermanence, emptiness, and Buddha-nature as the foundation of reality.

12. **Mahamudra and Dzogchen—The Path to Full Enlightenment** – The Four Yogas of Mahamudra and the Three Statements of Garab Dorje in Dzogchen guide the practitioner toward recognizing and stabilizing Awakened Awareness. These teachings nurture Awakening to full enlightenment.

13. **The Wisdom Energies and Buddha Bodies—The Unending Activity of Enlightenment** – The Five Wisdom Energies and Three Buddha Bodies reveal how enlightenment continuously expresses itself in the world through form and activity.

14. **Buddhahood as a Unique Expression—A Single Realization with a Rainbow of Expressions** – Every Buddha manifests uniquely as an emanation of one of the Five Archetypal Buddha Families.

15. **Completion and Compassion—The End of the Path, the Beginning of Buddhahood**– Although liberation comes to completion, refining skillful means and compassionate activity is endless.

Each of these dimensions weave seamlessly with the others, ensuring an enlightenment that is stable, integrated, and embodied.

## An Invitation to Walk This Path Together

The purpose of this book is to offer a living path with exercises and practices that you can apply to your own life right now. My hope is that this book serves as a lamp, illuminating the way forward.

In the next chapter, we will explore the first step on this path: recognizing the precious opportunity of this human life.

For now, I invite you to reflect on these questions:

- What is your deepest motivation for spiritual practice?

- Where are you in your own journey? Are you seeking relief, seeking wisdom, or seeking full realization?

- What obstacles do you feel are blocking your way?

*No matter where you are, the path is already unfolding beneath your feet. Let's walk it together.*

# Chapter 3

# THE PRECIOUS OPPORTUNITY OF HUMAN LIFE

## Recognizing the Rarity of This Life

At some point in life, we all encounter experiences that prompt us to step back and reflect. These moments can arise from loss, illness, retirement, personal crisis, or even profound experiences of joy and beauty. These moments shake us out of routine and force us to ask, What is this life really about? What truly matters? Perhaps we even begin asking the classic questions:

Who am I? Why am I here?

Buddhism teaches that recognizing the preciousness of human life is one of the first steps on the gradual path to Awakening. This realization isn't meant to create pressure or guilt but rather to shift our perspective, to help us see that we have a rare and valuable opportunity to live with awareness, purpose, and wisdom.

Many of us move through life as if we have endless time, as if we can get to the deeper questions *later*, after we've achieved success, built our families, or checked off all the boxes of societal expectations. But as we will explore in this chapter, postponing what matters most is one of the greatest risks we can take.

**Why This Life is an Extraordinary Opportunity**

The Buddhist teachings describe how rare it is to find yourself in a human life capable of spiritual practice. They say the chances of being born a human is comparable a blind turtle surfacing once every hundred years who happens to, by chance, poke its head through a golden ring floating on the surface of the ocean. In other words, all abstract visuals aside, a human life with all of the freedoms and advantages we currently find ourselves with, is rare.

But what makes human life so precious?

1. **We have the capacity for self-awareness.** Unlike beings driven purely by instinct, we can reflect on our experiences, make conscious choices, and cultivate wisdom.

2. **We have access to profound teachings.** Many people in the world do not have exposure to deep wisdom traditions, and even fewer have the time or resources to truly engage with them. Yet here we are, with the luxury to contemplate sacred teachings.

3. **We have the freedom to practice.** Unlike those in extreme suffering or oppression, we have the space to explore deeper questions about meaning and fulfillment. How fortunate!

4. **We have the urgency of impermanence.** Our lives are finite, making every moment an opportunity to engage with clarity and intention. If we lived forever, we might never get around to seeking answers to our deepest questions. But here we are, life is short!

Recognizing this doesn't mean we need to renounce everything or abandon worldly life. Rather, it invites us to bring more awareness into how we live.

## The Possibility of Awakening: Perhaps No One Ever Told You It Was Possible

Many people never explore the path of Awakening, not because they have rejected it, but because no one ever told them something called "Awakening" was even possible.

In my early 20's, I had my first taste of Awakening. It was profound and radically altered my life. It lasted for several months and then faded. The very first question I ever asked Dan Brown was, "Is it really possible to stabilize Awakening all of the time?" And he said, "Of course! That's the whole point!"

But up until that point in my life no one had ever told me that the stabilization of Awakening was the "whole point"! I had thought Awakening was more like a state that came and went. I hadn't yet considered the fact that Awakening was something that could be recognized all the time. Sometimes, we simply need to know what is possible.

So whether you already know it's true or are hearing it for the first time, I'm here to tell you that *enlightenment is possible*. And even more than that, enlightenment is possible not just in some future life but in this very life. In fact, that's the whole point! That's why you are here. That's why you are reading this book right now!

Choosing a life dedicated to Awakening is the most meaningful and fulfilling choice we can possibly make.

Think about this for a moment. How many people spend their entire lives believing that things simply are the way they are, assuming that their experience of the world is fixed and unchangeable? How many people struggle with suffering, anxiety, or restlessness, never realizing that there is an actual path to freedom? How many people move through life without ever being told that deep, lasting contentment is possible, not just for rare mystics, but for them, in this very life?

For most, the idea that profound transformation is available has never been presented as a reality. They were never shown that there is a way to see beyond the ordinary deluded mind, beyond struggle and confusion, into the vast freedom of Awakening.

But here is the truth: You do not have to live bound by limitation, stress, or unconscious patterns. There is something profoundly possible *for you*. Awakening is not just for monks, yogis, or saints. It is your birthright.

It is easy to assume that enlightenment is something abstract or far away. But every awakened being was once just like you, someone who questioned deeply, practiced sincerely, and ultimately discovered that liberation was real. *And if it was possible for them, it is possible for you.*

Right now, in this life, you have encountered the rarest of gifts: a human birth with the ability to reflect, practice, and transform. The teachings of Awakening are available to you in a pure form. The opportunity to step onto this path is not in some distant future, but now. This is the extraordinary opportunity that this life offers.

If you are reading these words, you have already glimpsed the door into deeper liberation and true fulfillment. Will you open it and walk through it?

## Integrating This Wisdom into Daily Life

Reflecting on the preciousness of life doesn't mean we need to make radical, immediate changes. Sometimes, small shifts in awareness have the greatest impact.

Here are three simple ways to cultivate a deeper recognition of this precious opportunity in daily life:

### 1. Morning Reflection: Each morning, take a moment to acknowledge:

> ◊ *"Today is a rare and precious day. I will use it wisely."*
> ◊ This small habit can shift your mindset from

autopilot to intentionality.

2. **Aligning with What Matters: Throughout the day, ask:**

   ◊ *"Is this action aligned with what I truly value?"*

   ◊ This question helps you navigate your decisions, from how you spend your time to how you engage with others.

1. **Cultivating Awareness in Small Moments:** We don't need hours of meditation to live consciously. Even small moments, such as pausing before speaking, fully experiencing a deep breath, appreciating the presence of a loved one, can help us wake up to the richness of life.

## Closing Reflection: Living with Purpose, Not Pressure

The goal of this contemplation is not to create more stress in your life. Instead, it cultivates gratitude and presence. When we deeply appreciate life, we naturally become more engaged, more awake, and more compassionate.

So I invite you to reflect:

   ◊ *What does living intentionally mean to you?*

   ◊ What small step can you take today to align your life with what truly matters?

In the next chapter, we will explore the truth of impermanence and the inevitability of death.

For now, simply remember:

*This life is rare. It is a precious opportunity to wake up.*

## Chapter 4

# IMPERMANENCE AND THE REALITY OF DEATH

## Embracing Change as the Heart of the Path

In the previous chapter, we explored the preciousness of human life, recognizing how rare and valuable this existence is. But an equally important realization follows: this life is not only rare, it is fleeting. If we do not deeply internalize the truth of impermanence, we risk losing our precious time to distraction, hesitation, and attachment to things that will inevitably change.

Impermanence is not an abstract philosophy, it is our direct experience in every moment. The body ages, relationships shift, emotions rise and fall, careers evolve, and everything we hold onto eventually transforms.

Yet, rather than seeing impermanence as a problem to be solved, we can come to understand that impermanence itself is what makes life meaningful. If everything were fixed, unchanging, and eternal, there would be no growth, no depth of experience, and no possibility of transformation.

The more we resist impermanence, the more we suffer. The more we open to it, the more we align with reality.

## The Two Faces of Impermanence

There are two ways to look at impermanence:

1. **The Aspect of Loss** – This is what we usually think of when we consider impermanence: the passing away of loved ones, the end of relationships, the loss of youth, and the dissolving of things we once thought were permanent. When approached with attachment, this side of impermanence can lead to grief, fear, and suffering.

2. **The Aspect of Possibility** – Impermanence is also what allows for healing, transformation, and growth. Because nothing is fixed, we are never stuck. Suffering is temporary, identities can evolve, and the conditions that hold us back today may change tomorrow. This is the liberating side of impermanence.

When we grasp both of these truths, we begin to see impermanence as neither good nor bad but it is simply the way things are. And within this truth, we have a choice: to either resist it and suffer or embrace it and find freedom.

## Death is Real, and Its Time is Uncertain

One of the most powerful reflections on impermanence is acknowledging the reality of our own death. Here is what we know to be true:

- **Death is certain**—every being that is born will eventually die. There is no exception.

- **The time of death is uncertain**—we do not know when, where, or how we will die.

- **At the time of death, nothing can be taken with us**—our possessions, status, and even the body itself must all be left behind.

Let's take this out of the abstract and bring it closer to home. This means that *your* own death is certain. You are going to die. The timing of your death is unknown. You have no idea when you will die. At death, you can't take anything with you.

This truth can be deeply unsettling, yet it is also one of the most profound teachers you will ever encounter.

Most of us live as if we have infinite time. We postpone what truly matters. We assume there will always be another day, another chance, another moment to do what we have been meaning to do. But the reality is that we have no idea when our last moment will come. Was last night's sunset the last we'll ever see? Was that the last time you'll ever tell your children you love them? If we are honest with ourselves, we really don't know.

Contemplating your own death is not meant to create anxiety but to cultivate clarity and urgency, a sense of focus on what truly matters.

When we embrace the reality of death, we stop postponing happiness, realizing that now is the only time to be fully alive. We release trivial concerns, no longer wasting energy on things that do not truly matter. We engage fully with life, knowing that each moment is precious and unrepeatable.

If we deeply understand that our own death is real and its time is uncertain, we will naturally turn toward what is most meaningful. Rather than wasting our time in distraction, hesitation, or regret, we'll use this precious opportunity of human life in a way that is deeply meaningful.

## Impermanence as a Gateway to Liberation

Overall, whether it's through the contemplation of death or simply a deeper relationship with change, understanding impermanence naturally leads to a more liberated way of being. With this understanding, life becomes fluid, responsive, and free from rigid attachments.

Ultimately, a deeper recognition of impermanence softens our grip on identity. Instead of clinging to fixed ideas about who we are, we begin to see ourselves as ever-evolving. Old self-concepts lose their hold, and we grant ourselves the freedom to grow, change, and unfold naturally, without the fear of losing something essential.

In relationships, this perspective brings a sense of openness and ease. Rather than trying to control others or expecting them to remain the same, we embrace the truth that all connections are dynamic and alive. We stop demanding permanence from those we love and instead meet them as they are in each moment, appreciating the beauty of their unfolding.

Endings, too, become less daunting. The closing of a chapter, the passing of a loved one, or the loss of something once cherished no longer needs to be met with fear or regret. When we recognize that everything arises and dissolves in its own time, we learn to greet transitions with acceptance and grace.

This is why the Buddhists do not instruct us to resist impermanence but to recognize its nature with openness and clarity.

Rather than struggling against the inevitable flow of life, we discover that embracing impermanence allows us to move with it effortlessly, finding freedom in the unfolding of each moment.

## Practices for Integrating Impermanence and Death into Daily Life

### 1. The Impermanence Journal

At the end of each day, take a few minutes to reflect:

◊ *What changed today?*

◊ *What was impermanent that I tried to hold onto?*

◊ *How did impermanence open up new possibilities today?*

By regularly noticing small impermanences, we prepare ourselves to meet larger changes with wisdom.

## 2. The Awareness of Breath

Sit for a few minutes and simply observe your breath. Each inhale arises and dissolves, making way for the next.

This is a direct experience of impermanence. As you breathe, get curious. Notice that no two breaths are the same, yet something within you remains steady, witnessing it all.

## 3. The Death Contemplation

Each morning, remind yourself:

◊ *I do not know if I will be alive tomorrow.*

◊ *What truly matters if today were my last?*

◊ *How can I live fully now, without regret?*

This practice cuts through distractions and reminds us to align our lives with what is most important.

## Closing Reflection: Flowing with Change, Embracing Life

Impermanence is not something we need to conquer, fix, or escape but it is something we must learn to dance with. The more we embrace change, the more we align with the flow of life itself.

Understanding impermanence naturally leads us to the next essential reflection: karma and cause and effect. If everything changes, then our actions can shape what arises next. How we live, how we think, and how we engage with the world creates the conditions for what unfolds.

In the next chapter, we will explore how karma provides a profound understanding of how we shape our own experience.

For now, simply remember:

*Death is real, its time is uncertain. Let this truth bring you fully into life.*

# Chapter 5

# KARMA AND THE POWER OF CAUSE AND EFFECT

## Shaping our Destiny Through Intentional Action

If impermanence teaches us that nothing stays the same, karma teaches us that nothing happens randomly. All of the moments of our experience, our emotions, thoughts, relationships, and even the circumstances of our lives, have been shaped by an intricate web of causes and conditions.

Karma, in its simplest definition, means cause and effect. It is the recognition that our actions, physical, emotional, and mental, set into motion a chain of consequences that shape our future. But karma is not fate, nor is it a system of divine judgment. It is a natural law, much like gravity, operating through patterns of habit, intention, and consequence.

Understanding karma teaches us to recognize that we are not powerless. Even though we cannot control everything that happens in life, we can consciously shape our future trajectory by how we think, speak, and act now.

## Karma Beyond the Superstition

Many people misunderstand karma. In popular

culture, karma is often reduced to a system of instant justice, as if doing something bad results in immediate misfortune or doing something good guarantees an immediate reward.

But karma doesn't work like a vending machine. It is more like planting seeds in a garden. Some seeds sprout quickly, while others take years to bear fruit. Some karmic seeds leave a very deep impression and, therefore, have a more substantial impact when they sprout. Other karmic seeds are planted in a very shallow way, and the impact they leave when they bear fruit is minimal. Our current life circumstances are shaped by both immediate and long-term causes, including from recent actions and others from patterns that have built up over time.

This is why life often seems unfair. People with good hearts sometimes suffer, while people who act selfishly seem to thrive. But the law of karma is not based on short-term appearances. Just as some plants take years to blossom, the effects of our actions often take time to unfold.

## The Four Aspects of Karma

In traditional Buddhist teachings, karma has four defining characteristics:

1. **Karma is certain.** Once an action is set into motion, its effects will follow unless counteracted by other causes. A seed that is planted will grow when conditions are right.

2. **Karma expands.** A small action can have rippling effects. A single act of kindness or harm can set off a chain of consequences far beyond what we can see.

3. **We only experience the results of our own karma.** As a general principle, the experiences we have result from the karmic seeds we've planted

through our own previous actions. Keep in mind that it may be skillful and compassionate to adapt the explanation of this aspect of karma in the context of those who have experienced traumatic events.

4. **Karma is not erased unless it ripens or is purified.** Actions leave lasting impressions in our consciousness. Without deliberate transformation, either through our own efforts or through the blessings of an enlightened being, negative patterns will continue to shape our experience.

These principles help us understand why we are where we are today, and, more importantly, how we can consciously shape where we are going.

## How Karma Shapes Our Mind and Identity

One of the most powerful aspects of karma is not just how it affects external circumstances but how it shapes our own minds: Every time we act with kindness, patience, or generosity, we strengthen those qualities within ourselves. Every time we act from anger, greed, or fear, we reinforce those tendencies as well.

An understanding of karma impacts how we respond to circumstances regardless of what is unfolding.

If we are not mindful, we might unconsciously repeat old patterns, such as reacting to situations in the same way, making the same choices, and recreating the same struggles. But the moment we bring awareness to our actions we gain the power to change.

## The Power of Intention

Not all actions carry the same weight in shaping karma. The intention behind an action is often more important than the action itself.

For example, accidentally stepping on an insect is different from intentionally harming one. Giving to charity out of love is different from giving to impress others. And speaking harshly out of anger is different from speaking strongly out of necessary compassion.

This means that karma is not just about what we do but about the energy behind our actions. When we cultivate skillful intentions that are infused with love, clarity, wisdom, we set in motion the causes for future well-being.

## Karma and Free Will: Are We Stuck in Our Patterns?

If our lives are shaped by past karma, does that mean we are simply prisoners of our past actions? Absolutely not.

The present moment is always a pivot point. No matter what patterns we have inherited, whether from past lives, childhood conditioning, or recent choices, we always have the ability to shift direction.

Imagine karma as a river flowing in a certain direction. If we do nothing, we are carried by the current of our past actions. But if we bring awareness and effort, we can begin to swim in a new direction.

This is why mindfulness is key. The more present we are, the more we can recognize old patterns as they arise and consciously choose a different response.

There is a famous saying often attributed to the great Dzogchen Master Padmasambhava. He says:

*"If you want to know your past life, look at your present condition; if you want to know your future life, look at your present actions."*

Padmasambhava's words of wisdom highlight the principle of cause and effect (karma) as it shapes our experiences across time. He teaches that our present circumstances, whether fortunate or challenging, are the direct result of our past actions. Likewise, the choices we make now determine the course of our future, both in this life and beyond.

This wisdom emphasizes personal responsibility, encouraging mindful action and ethical conduct as the foundation for a positive future. It reminds us that transformation is always within our hands, and by cultivating wisdom and compassion in the present, we can shape a more enlightened destiny.

So, rather than trying to predict or control karma, our task is simply this: to plant the best seeds possible, moment by moment, action by action, right now.

## Transforming Negative Karma

Because karma is not fate, we are never stuck with the consequences of past actions. There are even specific ways to purify and transform negative karma. Here is an example of four steps you can take to get yourself back on track:

1. **Recognition** – Acknowledging harmful actions we have done in the past without denial or self-judgment.

2. **Regret (Not Guilt)** – Feeling genuine remorse, not as self-punishment, but as motivation to change.

3. **Recommitment** – Making the decision not to repeat those actions.

4. **Restorative Action** – Engaging in positive actions that help balance and counteract past harm.

Let's look at the following example: if someone recognizes they have caused harm through harsh speech, they can acknowledge it (recognition), feel a desire to change (regret), decide not to act out with that kind of speech again (recommitment), and then consciously practice more kind and thoughtful speech going forward as a way to shift their karmic momentum (restorative action).

This method of behavior change is always possible, no matter who you are or what you've done in the past. Every instant is a new opportunity to plant positive karmic seeds.

Through awareness, intention, and effort, we can all learn to redirect our lives in profound ways.

## Engaging with Karma in Daily Life

Rather than seeing karma as some exotic spiritual force, we can bring it into practical, daily awareness. Here are three simple ways to work with karma:

### 1. The Three-Gate Reflection: Thought, Speech, Action

Before making a decision, ask:

◊ *Is this thought, word, or action beneficial or harmful?*

◊ *Does it come from wisdom or from habit?*

◊ *What seeds am I planting for my future self?*

This simple pause can transform reactivity into mindful action.

### 2. Observing Patterns Without Judgment

Pay attention to recurring themes in your life, whether in relationships, work, or emotional struggles. These patterns may reveal karmic tendencies. Instead of blaming external circumstances, explore:

◊ *How might my past actions, thoughts, or expectations be shaping this pattern?*

◊ *What can I do differently to shift this cycle?*

### 3. Planting Seeds of Positive Karma

Each day, make an effort to consciously plant good seeds through:

- **Small acts of kindness** (even a smile or a kind word).

- **Mindful speech** (avoiding gossip, speaking truthfully with compassion).

- **Engaging in generosity** (not just with money, but with time, attention, and care).

Over time, these small actions create a ripple effect of positive momentum.

## Closing Reflection: Taking Responsibility for Our Path

Ultimately, karma is about understanding our own power and agency. When we live unconsciously, we are swept along by our past conditioning. But when we become aware of karma, we step into the role of conscious actors.

This chapter is not meant to make you feel burdened by past actions, but rather empowered to shape your present and future life.

So, I invite you to reflect:

◊ *What patterns are you unconsciously repeating?*

◊ *What seeds do you want to plant for your future self?*

◊ *How can you bring more mindfulness into your daily choices?*

In the next chapter, we will explore the nature of suffering: what it truly is, why it exists, and how we can move beyond it.

For now, simply remember:

*Every thought, word, and action shapes your path. This moment is an opportunity to plant positive karmic seeds for the future.*

Chapter 6

# UNDERSTANDING SUFFERING

## The Cause of Suffering and Its End

Suffering is an undeniable part of human existence. It manifests as physical pain, emotional distress, existential uncertainty, and a subtle unease that lingers even in moments of happiness. In Buddhist teachings, this is called dukkha or a fundamental dissatisfaction woven into conditioned reality. The experience that life is full of suffering in the way it is usually lived is the First Noble Truth in Buddhism.

But just like karma, suffering is not an unchangeable fate. It arises due to causes and conditions. And because it has a cause, it can be understood, transformed, and ultimately transcended.

### The Three Types of Suffering

The historical Buddha described three levels of suffering:

1. **The Suffering of Suffering** – The most direct form of suffering, encompassing physical pain, emotional distress, illness, grief, and hardship.

2. **The Suffering of Change** – The reality that all pleasure is fleeting. Joyful moments, success, and love are all subject to impermanence, leading to sorrow when they inevitably shift.

### 3. The Suffering of Conditioned Existence

The most subtle suffering, the persistent restlessness arising from our attachment to a fixed sense of self and resistance to impermanence. Even when life appears perfect, an underlying instability remains.

While these forms of suffering are universal, they are not inescapable. The Buddha's great insight was that suffering arises from specific causes, which means it can be uprooted at its source.

## The Cause of Suffering: Reactivity

As stated above, the First Noble Truth is that life, as normally lived, is full of suffering and dissatisfaction (*dukkha*). The Second Noble Truth teaches that suffering is not simply an inevitable feature of life; it has a cause.

*The cause of suffering is reactivity.* The cause of our suffering is our conditioned responses to experience.

At any given moment, when we are operating out of ordinary awareness, we engage with reality in one of three ways:

1. **Attachment** – When we enjoy something, we try to hold onto it and try to make more of it.

2. **Aversion** – When we dislike something, we push it away and try to make less of it.

3. **Ignorance** – When we disengage from the present moment, lost in avoidance or delusion, we miss what's happening altogether.

These three patterns of reactivity (attachment, aversion, and ignorance) are the root of all suffering.

But there is another way.

## The Fourth Possibility: Meeting Experience with Pure Awareness

Meditation practice teaches us a radical alternative to our habitually reactive way of being: instead of reacting to experience, *we can meet it with pure awareness.* This means observing sensations, emotions, and thoughts without grasping, resisting, or turning away. In this way we meet our experiences with perfect equanimity. When we cultivate this open presence toward our experience, suffering begins to dissolve. When we meet experience with pure, non-reactive awareness, we are no longer caught in the struggle to control what cannot be controlled.

While the First Noble Truth articulates the truth of suffering, and the Second Noble Truth describes its cause, the Third Noble Truth states that suffering has an end. Meeting each experience with pure awareness is the key to ending the cycle of reactivity and suffering.[1]

### Practical Ways to Work with Suffering

Instead of trying to escape suffering, we can turn toward it with awareness and skillfulness. Here are three practical approaches for you to try:

### 1. The Practice of Witnessing

- When suffering arises, instead of reacting, simply observe:

    ◊ *Where do I feel this in my body?*

    ◊ *What thoughts are attached to this feeling?*

    ◊ *What happens when I allow it to be here without resisting it?*

---

1. We'll talk about seeing through suffering using the lens of emptiness in more detail in Chapter 13 in our discussion on insight meditation.

- This practice creates space between experience and reaction, weakening suffering's grip.

- As a result, you can learn to respond with intention rather than react out of habit.

## 2. Shifting from Resistance to Curiosity

- Instead of saying, "Why is this happening to me?," ask:

  ◊ *"What is this teaching me?"*

  ◊ *"How can I meet this with openness rather than contraction?"*

  ◊ *Suffering often contains hidden wisdom because when we stop resisting it, we can access its lessons.*

## 3. Practicing Non-Reactivity, Not Indifference

Try meeting all experiences with pure, nonreactive awareness. Just be fully present with whatever is occurring. This kind of even-mindedness allows us to meet life fully without reactivity. But be careful! Many people mistake non-reactivity for indifference. Non-reactivity and indifference are profoundly different states of being.

**Indifference** is a withdrawal from life. It is a shutting down of emotions, a disengagement from relationships, experiences, and responsibilities. It arises from avoidance, fear, or apathy, leading to a sense of detachment that numbs both joy and suffering.

**Non-reactivity,** on the other hand, is a deep engagement with life without being bound by it. It is the ability to love wholeheartedly without clinging, to take action without rigid expectations, and to experience both joy and sorrow without becoming enslaved by either.[2]

Buddhism advocates the Middle Way, which involves living with presence and openness, yet remaining

---

2. We explore the differences between these two ways of being in more detail in Chapter 9 in our discussion around equanimity.

deeply intimate and in contact with all of experience.

## Closing Reflection: Turn Suffering into Liberation

The truth of suffering is not meant to depress us; it is meant to wake us up.

Suffering is the mind's way of pointing out where we are clinging, resisting, or caught in illusion. When we see suffering clearly, it becomes a teacher, not an enemy.

So, I invite you to reflect:

◊ *Where in your life do you struggle most with suffering?*

◊ *What are you grasping onto that is causing you pain?*

◊ *How would it feel to loosen your grip, just a little?*

In the next chapter, we will explore the reality of the Fourth Noble Truth: there is a path that leads to the end of suffering. The path beyond suffering begins with taking refuge, committing to that which can truly bring lasting fulfillment.

For now, simply remember:

*Suffering is not a punishment. It is an invitation to wake up. Begin by meeting all experiences with pure awareness.*

Chapter 7

# FINDING TRUE REFUGE

## Resting in What is Unshakable

In the last chapter, we explored suffering , its causes, and that suffering has an end. These are the First, Second, and Third Noble Truths of Buddhism. Now, we take the next step: discovering the reality of the Fourth Noble Truth. The Fourth Noble Truth states that there is a path beyond suffering. The path beyond suffering begins with discovering and committing to that which can bring true and lasting fulfillment. In Buddhism, we call this taking refuge.

Refuge in Buddhism refers to the inner shelter we turn to amidst the storms of suffering, uncertainty, and impermanence. It's not about avoiding difficult circumstances but rather about finding stability even while in the midst of life's challenges. Refuge is like taking shelter in a vast, unshakable sanctuary within our own mind and in our own heart. True refuge is the realization that peace and freedom are not found outside ourselves but within the clarity and openness of our own awakened nature.

### False Refuge

At some point in life, we reach a turning point, a moment when we realize that the strategies we've relied on to find happiness aren't working. We recognize we've been caught up in a kind of false refuge. A false refuge is anything impermanent that we cling to for security, happiness, or identity but which ultimately cannot provide lasting fulfillment or freedom.

These places of false refuge may provide temporary relief, but they ultimately fail to address the root of suffering. Instead of leading to lasting peace, they keep us caught in cycles of grasping, avoidance, and ignorance.

Some of the most common areas of life where people take false refuge include:

- **Material wealth** – Money provides security, but not inner peace. Even with financial stability, anxiety, dissatisfaction, and impermanence remain.

- **Romantic relationships** – Love is beautiful, but no person can resolve our deepest existential restlessness. Seeking wholeness through another can lead to attachment, dependency, and inevitable disappointment when relationships change.

- **Status and reputation** – Praise feels good, but is fleeting and conditional. The constant need for approval and recognition only reinforces egoic insecurity rather than true confidence.

- **Intellectual knowledge** – Understanding concepts does not automatically lead to transformation. Without direct experience, even the most profound teachings remain theoretical rather than lived wisdom.

- **Pleasure and distraction** – Enjoyment fades and avoidance only postpones suffering. Seeking refuge in entertainment or indulgence numbs discomfort but does not resolve its cause.

None of these things are inherently bad. The problem is when we treat them as our ultimate refuge; we expect them to provide a kind of stability that they simply cannot offer.

For those already well on their way on the spiritual path, there are a few additional forms of false refuge that may arise which are worth mentioning.

## False Refuge in Inner Work

While psychological healing is a crucial aspect of the path, it can also become a false refuge when it replaces rather than supports true Awakening. Some practitioners become endlessly preoccupied with inner work, such as healing trauma, analyzing childhood wounds, or refining personality structures, yet without ever stepping beyond the self-improvement paradigm into deeper liberation.

Inner work is not the same as enlightenment. Psychological wholeness can bring greater ease and integration, but without a larger context of wisdom and Awakening, it can become another form of self-fixation. True refuge goes beyond working on the self because it involves seeing through the self altogether.

With that said, neglecting psychological work in the name of spiritual transcendence is also a mistake.

True spiritual health includes both:

1. **Relative Wholeness** – Integrating wounds, healing attachments, and cultivating emotional maturity all help to create a healthy sense of self. This is cleaning up.

2. **Unbounded Wholeness** – Recognizing the illusory nature of the self and resting in the vast boundless nature of awareness itself. This is waking up.

Relative wholeness without unbounded wholeness has no freedom or liberation. It can lead to burnout and exhaustion.

Unbounded wholeness without relative wholeness leaves the self fractured. It can set the conditions for harmful conduct in the world.

We've all heard stories of spiritual teachers who may have genuine access to Awakening (unbounded wholeness) but an underdeveloped relative self structure (lack relative wholeness). The stories about abuse of power and sexual misconduct that follow this dangerous recipe should be a warning sign for us all.

As we'll see in the later chapters, a lack of integration in this way is one of the critical differences between a fully enlightened Buddha (a true Guru) and a spiritual teacher who is not yet fully developed. A full Buddha's conduct in the world always leaves a trail of goodness. A partially enlightened being can still do harm. I mention this explicitly so that we do not throw out the baby with the bathwater. Let us not dismiss the reality of fully Enlightened teachers because of the fact that some partially enlightened teachers do harm.

When the two dimensions of unbounded wholeness and relative wholeness are balanced, the path becomes grounded, holistic, and sustainable. We need both *waking up* and *cleaning up* for true spiritual wholeness

.

## False Refuge in Service to Others

Another place where more advanced practitioners may find false refuge is in service to others. While service and generosity are essential aspects of the awakened heart, they can also become a subtle avoidance when they are used in place of genuine realization. Some people dedicate themselves to philanthropy, activism, or humanitarian work, yet remain inwardly unfulfilled because they have not addressed their own suffering, attachments, or blind spots. Some people might even find themselves in the role of a spiritual teacher or community leader doing good and noble work, but when this drive comes from unconscious patterns of wanting to be seen, liked, or admired, it can lead to burnout and resentment.

Giving back is beautiful and necessary, but it is not a substitute for Awakening. When service comes from a place of seeking validation, guilt, or avoidance of self-inquiry, it can become another form of external refuge. When it arises naturally from realization, it is the effortless expression of wisdom and compassion. It's vital to know the difference.

## Turning from False Refuge to True Refuge

Objects of false refuge are not inherently negative since wealth, love, knowledge, healing, and service all have their place. The problem arises when we cling to them as sources of ultimate security. True refuge is not found in external conditions, rather it is found in Awakening to the nature of our own mind. *The only true refuge is Awakening.*

By recognizing where we seek refuge in places that may not be ultimately fulfilling, we can start to distinguish that which is worthy of true refuge.

In Buddhism, we express taking refuge in Awakening through the Three Jewels: The Buddha, Dharma, and Sangha. We take refuge in the Buddha (our awakened potential), the Dharma (the path to realization), the Sangha (the support of spiritual community). The Three Jewels are the support needed to awaken.

At a certain point in our own spiritual evolution, we discover that only in this living refuge of the Three Jewels can we find the deep, unshakable peace that nothing in the conditioned world can provide. Refuge in the Buddha, Dharma, and Sangha shows us the path and support we need to wake up.

For any of you reading this book who don't consider yourself Buddhist, there's an important point that I'd like to make here. Taking refuge in the Three Jewels of Buddha, Dharma, Sangha, is not about promoting Buddhism as the only way. The principles behind these three jewels are what's important. And these principles are universal. For Christians, the Buddha could be Jesus, the Dharma could be the Bible, and the Sangha could be the church. The essence of refuge is what matters. True refuge is about acknowledging your own potential, recognizing a path, and finding a community to support your Awakening. While this book focuses on Buddhism, the deeper invitation here is to engage with these timeless truths in a way that resonates with your own path.

## The Living Refuge: Buddha, Dharma, Sangha, and the Role of the Lama

Taking refuge in the Three Jewels—Buddha, Dharma, and Sangha—is the foundation of the Buddhist spiritual path. Each jewel serves as a guide, protector, and source of Awakening, but their significance evolves as one's practice deepens.

## The Dharma: The Path to Awakening

For many, Dharma is the first and most immediate refuge. Buddhist teachings (and sacred teachings from other traditions) show us another way of living beyond convention. In a Buddhist context, the teachings illuminate suffering, impermanence, emptiness, and the nature of mind. In this way, the Dharma provides a clear method for transformation, guiding us through:

- **Ethical conduct** to purify harmful habits.

- **Meditation** to cultivate a calm, stable mind.

- **Wisdom** to see through illusion and recognize our true nature.

However, while the Dharma is the map, it is not the journey itself. True understanding of the Dharma comes not from reading texts or intellectual study but from direct experience.

## The Buddha: The Embodiment of Awakening

The realization that intellectual study is not enough reinforces the need for the second jewel: the Buddha. At the beginning of the path, we may look to the historical Buddha as an external example, but as insight deepens, we see that Buddhahood is our own deepest nature. To take refuge in the Buddha means to commit to realizing Buddhahood within ourselves in our own direct experience.

Exposure to the Dharma inspires us to reach our own highest potential. The historical Buddha, Shakyamuni, exemplifies this realization, showing that freedom from suffering is possible. Ultimately, however, the Buddha is not just a historical figure but is the awakened nature present in all beings, waiting to be fully realized.

## The Sangha: Walking the Path Together

When we get serious about bringing the realizations into our own direct experience, we realize how valuable it can be to travel the path with others. Taking refuge in the Sangha means committing to the community of practitioners who support and embody the path. Spiritual practice is not meant to be walked alone, therefore, the Sangha provides:

- **Encouragement and accountability** when challenges arise.
- **Collective wisdom** from those further along the path.
- **A field of shared merit** that accelerates Awakening.

The Sangha helps dissolve self-centeredness, reinforcing the reality of interconnection and compassion. Through the Sangha, we learn that our Awakening is not separate from the Awakening of others. Our practice is for the benefit of all beings. As insight deepens, we begin to realize that all of relative reality is the sangha. Everything is a teaching, everyone is part of our sacred community, helping us along the path.

Taking refuge in the three jewels of Buddha, Dharma, Sangha is vital. But it is also incredibly meaningful to realize that direct experience can be greatly enhanced through the guidance of a living teacher or mentor (the Lama).

## The Lama: The Living Bridge Between Buddha, Dharma, and Sangha

The direct translation of the word *Lama* is quite wonderful. In Tibetan, the syllable "La" refers to soul, essence, or intrinsic presence, while "Ma" means mother. So *Lama* can be directly translated as "Soul Mother," reflecting the profound, nurturing role a teacher plays on the spiritual path. This phrase captures something more than the English word mentor or teacher. The word Lama symbolizes the role of a compassionate guide who births the student into awakened awareness.

Just as a mother brings a child into the world and nourishes its growth, the Lama transmits wisdom, nurtures realization, and protects the disciple from veering off the path, offering both tender care and fierce guidance to ensure spiritual maturation. In Mahamudra and Dzogchen, this soul-mother relationship is the heart of direct realization, for it is through the Lama's blessing, pointing-out instructions, and unwavering presence that the student awakens to their own Buddha-nature.

While the Buddha provides the original example,

the Dharma offers the path, and the Sangha reinforces it all, it is through the Lama that these Three Jewels become fully alive in direct experience.

## Why the Lama is Even More Important Than the Buddha

At the beginning of the path, the Buddha seems like the ultimate refuge, after all, he's the enlightened one who figured it all out! But as practice deepens, the Tibetan teachings describe that something unexpected happens: the Lama becomes even more important than the historical Buddha.

Why? Well, for starters:

- **The historical Buddha is distant, but the Lama is here now**—offering wisdom and guidance.

- **The Dharma is vast and complex, but the Lama makes it immediate**—cutting through confusion with teachings tailored to exactly what you need in a simple and direct way.

- **The Sangha provides companionship, but the Lama delivers realization**—pointing out mind's nature with precision, like a spiritual GPS recalibrating every time you get lost.

In the highest teachings of Tibetan Buddhism there is a practice called Guru Yoga. Guru Yoga is a practice of devotion expressed toward the lama. But this practice isn't about idolizing a person; it's a direct method to dissolve the illusion of separation and recognize your own awakened nature. Ultimately, the guru is everywhere, expressing through everything, and a constant reminder to deepen the realization and to stay on the path.

The Lama is not separate from the Buddha, Dharma, or Sangha but is the living, breathing presence of all three, appearing as a fallible human who drinks tea, cracks bad jokes, and occasionally still forgets to unmute when you are meeting with them on zoom.

## Refuge as a Living Relationship

One understanding I hope you've gathered from this chapter is that taking refuge is not a one-time decision. It is a learned way of being that deepens over time. In the beginning, we rely on the Dharma to open up the possibility of the path. As we deepen the journey, we take refuge in the Buddha as an external example and then in our own Buddha-Nature as our innate potential. Then, as we continue to mature, we find strength in Sangha, walking the path alongside others; inspiring each other to find our way home. Eventually, we recognize the Lama as the expression of all three, leading us to direct realization.

We start off the path by taking refuge in these precious jewels. *Overtime, as our realization matures, we become a refuge-being in whom others can take refuge.*

## Practicing Refuge in Daily Life

Taking refuge is not just a ceremonial act but is something we return to again and again in daily life. The Buddha, Dharma, Sangha, (and Lama) are living guides that we can lean on in every moment. Here's how to actively practice taking refuge:

### 1. Turning Toward our Awakened Mind

When facing difficulty, instead of reacting with fear or avoidance, ask:

"What would my most awakened self do in this moment? What would my teachers or mentors point out to me right now?"

Trust that beneath all confusion, you already have a capacity for wisdom and compassion; your teachers are there to remind you when you forget.

2. **Aligning with the Path**

When making decisions, reflect:

"Is this action leading me toward liberation, or deeper into attachment?"

The Dharma provides the roadmap, but the teacher or mentor makes sure you're reading the signs correctly. They will offer a well-placed question, a direct pointing-out instruction, or (when necessary) a compassionate but no-nonsense reality check.

3. **Seeking Support and Connection**

Engage with spiritual friends, teachers, and like-minded practitioners who uplift and support your path. If no immediate community is available, take refuge in the wisdom of sacred texts, recorded teachings, and reflections. And if you're lucky enough to have an authentic teacher or lama, remember: they are your personal connection to all three refuges, a bridge between conceptual understanding and direct experience. Don't give away your power but also be open enough to receive the blessings the lama holds.

Each time we consciously choose to turn toward these sources of true refuge, we strengthen the foundation of our practice by grounding ourselves in the living presence of wisdom, rather than the fleeting distractions of the conditioned world.

**Closing Reflection: Where Do You Take Refuge?**

As you reflect on this chapter, consider:

- Where have you been seeking false refuge in ways that do not provide lasting contentment?

- What would it mean to take refuge in something deeper, wiser, and more liberating?

- How can you make taking refuge a daily practice, rather than a one-time decision?

In the next chapter, we will explore ethics as the natural expression of walking the path with integrity and alignment.

For now, simply remember:

*Refuge is the active process of discovering and prioritizing that which can actually lead to lasting fulfillment.*

Chapter 8

# Living an Ethical Life

## Growing Up and Showing Up

In the previous chapter, we explored taking refuge. We discussed the fact that a meaningful and awakened life cannot be built on seeking lasting fulfillment through fleeting things like wealth, status, or external validation. Instead, take refuge in the awakened mind, the path of truth, and supportive community.

Finding true refuge is a commitment that transforms how we live. It shows up in our own attitude and equally as important, this radical shift shows up in our conduct. Ethics is where our practice moves beyond personal insight and into embodied action. Ethics is how we bring our realizations and new orientations to life into the world.

However, ethics can be misunderstood. Ethics is often seen as a rigid set of rules, imposed from outside, dictating what is "right" and "wrong." But in the way that I've learned it, Buddhist ethics is not about obedience but is about *alignment*. It is about living in harmony with reality, freeing ourselves from unnecessary suffering, and cultivating a way of being that supports both our liberation and the well-being of others.

This is where the dimensions of *growing up* and *showing up* become essential.

- **Growing up:** We all grow through predictable stages of development and maturity. In the case of ethics, this means developing a mature, developmentally-informed approach that evolves beyond blind rule-following into wisdom-based discernment.

- **Showing up:** Our internal commitments need to show up in our conduct. This means bringing ethical clarity into our daily interactions, ensuring that our conduct is an expression of Awakening rather than a contradiction of it.

## Growing Up: Ethics Through the Lens of Development

Just as our understanding of the world evolves as we mature, so too does our sense of right action. Ethics is not static but grows with us. I review four stages of ethical development below:

1. **Traditional Ethics: Morality as Obedience**

   - Based on external rules, commandments, and cultural norms.

   - Focused on duty, purity, and maintaining order.

   - Ethics is often fear-based, grounded in avoiding punishment or gaining rewards.

2. **Modern Ethics: Morality as Autonomy**

   - Based on reason, individual rights, and personal choice.

   - Seeks fairness and justice but can overemphasize personal freedom at the expense of interconnectedness.

3. **Postmodern Ethics: Morality as Contextual**

   - Recognizes that morality and ethics are shaped

by culture, history, and power dynamics.

- Values inclusivity and multiple perspectives but sometimes struggles with relativism, making ethical clarity difficult.

## 4. Integral Ethics: Morality as Wisdom

- Balances universal ethical principles with the ability to adapt to circumstances.

- Transcends both rigid rule-following and moral ambiguity, cultivating a wisdom-based, compassion-driven approach to ethics.

A developmentally mature ethical framework allows us to see beyond rigid categories of "good" and "bad" while avoiding the pitfalls of moral relativism. We recognize that ethical clarity is not about following rules but is about being deeply attuned to life itself.

This is the growing up aspect of ethics: moving beyond rule-based morality into a dynamic, wisdom-based engagement with reality.

## Showing Up: Ethics as the Expression of Awakening

Once we have developed a mature understanding of ethics, we must embody it in our actions. Ethical integrity is not about suppressing desires or conforming to an external code. Buddhist ethics is about acting in a way that supports Awakening rather than reinforcing suffering for ourselves and others.

Buddhist ethics traditionally emphasizes three levels of conduct:

## 1. Ethics of Restraint (Avoiding Harm)

- Refraining from actions that create suffering for ourselves and others.

- Includes restrain from lying, sexual misconduct,

and having ill intentions.

2. **Ethics of Cultivation (Actively Generating Well-Being)**

   • Going beyond avoiding harm to actively practicing virtues like generosity, kindness, and patience.

3. **Ethics of Wisdom (Responding with Insight)**

   • Understanding that no ethical rule is absolute recognizes that the most compassionate response requires flexibility.

   • For example, generosity is a virtue, but if giving money to someone struggling with addiction would enable self-harm, wisdom calls for offering support in a way that truly benefits them, such as providing food or access to resources instead.

When ethics is lived from wisdom rather than rules, it becomes a natural expression of Awakening rather than an imposed obligation.

## Contemporary Ethics: Personal Morality, Inner Work and Social Responsibility

In today's world, a fully integrated ethical life weaves together at least three essential threads: personal morality, inner psychological work, and social responsibility. We discussed personal morality above. Let's now turn to inner work and social responsibility.

## Inner Work & Psychological Wholeness

Ethics is not merely about our behavior in the moment, it is about how we actively participate in who we are becoming. Our unconscious fears, traumas, and conditioning do not remain locked within us; they find expression in our relationships and in the cultures we help shape. Without internal work, our unexamined wounds inevitably seep into the communities we lead, influencing the systems we create and perpetuating cycles of harm.

If we do not engage in deep inner work, our ethics will always be fragile, prone to distortion by hidden wounds and unmet needs.

For example, a leader who has never processed their own experiences of neglect may unconsciously seek validation through power, making decisions that serve ego rather than collective well-being. A parent who has not healed their own childhood wounds may unknowingly impose the same fears, anxieties, or rigid expectations onto their children. A spiritual teacher who has not faced their own shadows may create a toxic community where their unresolved authority issues manifest as control, manipulation, or abuse.

Without integration, these patterns continue unchecked, shaping the next generation and embedding dysfunction into the structures we build. Healing is not just personal but it is intergenerational and systemic. This is why inner work is not optional; it is a moral obligation for anyone who seeks to live ethically.

## Social Responsibility

Ethical living involves actively contributing to the well-being of the larger systems in which we participate. When we integrate our inner work with outer service, our ethical life expands beyond individual morality to collective flourishing. This means not just practicing kindness, but addressing the root causes of suffering in our communities and on our planet. It means not just avoiding exploitation, but using our resources and influence to uplift others who don't have access or platforms through which they express. It means not just seeking enlightenment for ourselves, but ensuring that pathways to Awakening are available to everyone, regardless of their social status or financial means.

A truly ethical life is engaged. It recognizes that our inner healing and social responsibility are inseparable. This is the essence of *showing up*: living with awareness, acting with compassion, and creating systemic change where each of us and our planet can thrive.

## The Freedom of Ethical Living

Many people resist ethics, believing it to be a restriction on freedom. In reality, however, it's all about alignment. Unethical actions create inner turmoil. Ethical actions lead to profound inner peace.

Deception traps a person in a web of their own making. Someone who lies must constantly manage their fabrications, living in fear of being exposed. Craving fuels an endless cycle of dissatisfaction no matter how much pleasure is attained, it is never enough. Anger binds a person in conflict, keeping them in a state of perpetual struggle.

In contrast, a life of ethical integrity brings an effortless sense of ease. Someone who lives ethically moves through the world without the weight of guilt or self-doubt. They trust themselves, knowing that their actions align with their values. They sleep peacefully, unburdened by regret or unresolved conflict. Their relationships unfold with openness and sincerity, free from manipulation or hidden agendas.

Ultimately, ethics creates the foundation for a stable, joyful, and awakened life.

## Practicing Ethics in Daily Life

Here are two practical ways to integrate ethics into daily life:

## 1. Examining Our Motivations

- At the end of each day, reflect:
- "Where did I act from wisdom?"
- "Where did I act from reactivity?"
- This practice builds self-awareness and gradual ethical refinement.

## 2. Committing to One Ethical Shift

- Choose one ethical area to focus on for a month.
- It could be practicing more mindful speech, being more generous, or responding with patience instead of reactivity.
- Approach it not as a rule, but as an experiment in self-liberation.

Over time, this approach transforms ethics from an obligation into a source of strength, clarity, and ease.

## Closing Reflection: Ethics as the Foundation for Awakening

Ethics is how Awakening is expressed in action.

Ethics is the bridge between our deepest realizations and the way we live. Ethics is how we walk the path. Without ethics, spirituality can become a form of bypassing or a way to seek Awakening while avoiding responsibility. But when ethical clarity is present, practice transforms into a fully lived expression. It becomes a path that not only deepens personal Awakening but also serves as a force of benefit for the world.

So I invite you to reflect:

- Where do you feel most aligned with ethical living?
- Where do you struggle? What keeps you from

acting with integrity?

• How would your life feel different if you lived
  with greater ethical clarity?

Dan Brown used to say, "Ultimately, the only way to
truly judge whether a person's realization is authentic or
not is through their conduct."

Authentic realizers have a positive influence on the
people around them. They leave a trail of goodness
wherever they go.

In the next chapter, we will explore the Four Immeasurables as a way to cultivate virtue and to show up
with the boundless qualities of an awakened heart.

For now, simply remember:

*Ethics is not about limitation—it is about alignment with
the way things truly are.*

# Chapter 9

# THE FOUR IMMEASURABLES

## The Boundless Qualities of an Awakened Heart

In the previous chapter, we explored the role of ethics as one of the foundational building blocks of the spiritual path. Ethical conduct is not merely about avoiding harm but it is about actively cultivating the conditions for Awakening. By aligning our actions with wisdom and compassion, we purify negative karma and accumulate positive merit, creating the inner stability needed for deeper transformation.

The next essential aspect of the path is learning how to cultivate virtuous qualities intentionally and consistently. The heart, like the mind, can be trained to expand into its fullest potential. In this chapter, we introduce the Four Immeasurables. These Four Immeasurables are: Unwavering Equanimity, Unconditional Love, Boundless Compassion, and Immeasurable Joy.

These four boundless qualities—Equanimity, Love, Compassion, and Joy—teach us how to train our heart. They help us transcend personal bias and self-interest. They train us to relate to all beings with openness, care, and delight, dissolving the illusion that some beings are more deserving of love than others.

Of course, these four virtues are not the only positive qualities worth cultivating. There is extensive contemporary research focused on the benefits of cultivating positivity. Barbara Fredrickson's research on positive emotions identifies additional qualities that contribute to human flourishing. In her work, she includes gratitude, awe, hope, and inspiration, among others. Similarly, Martin Seligman and Christopher Peterson, in their work on the VIA Classification of Character Strengths, outline a broader framework of virtues that support psychological well-being and ethical living. These virtues include wisdom, courage, justice, and temperance. Many other traditions, both spiritual and psychological, highlight countless additional virtues that contribute to a meaningful life.

For the purposes of this chapter, however, we focus on the Four Immeasurables. These are the four core virtues emphasized most extensively across nearly all Buddhist traditions. They are a good starting place, in part, because they are remarkably difficult to argue against. Who wouldn't agree that cultivating more equanimity, love, compassion, and joy is beneficial?

The Four Immeasurables are named as such because each of the qualities is boundless and immeasurable. There are no limits to them. In addition, it is said that the number of beings who benefit through their cultivation are immeasurable. No matter how much these qualities are cultivated, their value never diminishes but only deepens.

Just as ethical conduct provides a stable foundation for Awakening, the Four Immeasurables cultivate a vast, inclusive heart that begins to approximate an awakened mind. Together, ethics and the Four Immeasurables prepare the ground for the step we'll take together in the next chapter: Bodhicitta is the deep commitment to Awakening for the benefit of all beings.

## Why Tibetan Traditions Place Equanimity First

In many Buddhist traditions, the Four Immeasurables are presented in a sequence that begins with Unconditional Love (*Mettā/Maitri*), followed by Compassion (*Karuṇā*), Sympathetic Joy (*Muditā*), and Equanimity (*Upekshā*). This order reflects what may feel like a very natural progression starting with love and gradually expanding it into an all-encompassing, stable, and impartial state.

However, there are many examples in the Tibetan tradition that begin with Equanimity rather than Love. This shift in emphasis arises from the understanding that without equanimity, our love, compassion, and joy remain bound by bias and personal attachment.

Equanimity dissolves preferences and prejudices, leading to a vast, unbiased expression of the other three immeasurables. When we cultivate equanimity first, we train ourselves to see all beings as equally deserving of care without favoring friends over strangers or resisting those who challenge us. This unshakable openness then serves as the foundation for the other Immeasurables. With equanimity:

- **Love becomes more unconditional,** not just directed toward those who please us.

- **Compassion becomes universal and inexhaustible,** not swayed by personal attachment or burnout.

- **Sympathetic Joy becomes authentic,** celebrating others' happiness without comparison or envy.

By placing equanimity first, Tibetan teachings ensure that our love, compassion, and joy are free from grasping and aversion, making them truly boundless.

Each of the Four Immeasurables has both a far enemy (its direct opposite) and a near enemy (a subtle distortion that mimics it but is actually harmful). Recognizing these helps us cultivate genuine qualities rather than falling into their deceptive imitations.

We'll explore each of the Four Immeasurables along with their near and far enemies next.

## The Four Immeasurables

### 1. Equanimity (*Upekshā*) – The Foundation of Non-Reactivity and Evenness

Equanimity is the ability to meet all beings and experiences with evenness, free from excessive attachment or aversion. It is a vast, stable openness that allows all positive qualities to flow without bias. In simple terms, equanimity is a kind of nonreactivity.

In many ways, equanimity is the culmination of a stable mind, the natural result of ethical conduct and meditative training. A mind without equanimity is tossed around by circumstances, reacting impulsively to pleasure and pain, praise and blame, success and failure.

True equanimity does not dull the heart but it refines it. It allows us to care deeply, to be intimate with life, without being consumed by attachment or aversion.

## The Near and Far Enemies of Equanimity

- **Far Enemy: Reactivity**—Being overwhelmed by emotions, easily swayed by circumstances, treating some beings as more worthy of care than others.

- **Near Enemy: Indifference/Apathy**— Appearing "calm" but actually emotionally withdrawn, suppressing feelings rather than transforming them.

## Practicing Equanimity

- **Reflect:** "All beings, including myself, experience both joy and suffering. No one is exempt."

- **Notice** where you treat some people as more "worthy" of love than others.

- **Contemplate:** *"Just as I wish to be happy, so do all beings."*

Equanimity dissolves preferences and prejudices, leading to a vast, unbiased love that can hold both pain and beauty with equal grace.

### 2. Unconditional Love (*Mettā/Maitri*) – The Wish for All Beings to Be Happy

Unconditional love (*Metta/Maitri*), sometimes called loving-kindness, is the active wish for all beings to experience happiness and well-being. Unlike equanimity, which focuses on evenness and nonreactivity, unconditional love is radiant and expansive.

It does not depend on whether someone "deserves" love. It is not about liking or approving of others; it is about recognizing their shared longing for happiness and truly wishing that for them.

## The Near and Far Enemies of Unconditional Love

- **Far Enemy: Hatred**—The desire to harm or reject others.

- **Near Enemy:** Conditional or self-centered love—Love that is possessive, transactional, or based on personal gratification rather than genuine care.

## Practicing Unconditional Love

A simple yet profound method is a Loving-Kindness Meditation:

1. Start with yourself: *"May I be happy. May I be safe. May I be free from suffering."*

2. Extend to a loved one: *"May you be happy. May you be safe. May you be free from suffering."*

3. Extend to a neutral person (someone you do not know well).

4. Extend to a difficult person (someone you struggle with).

5. Expand to all beings everywhere.

Through this practice, we train the heart to soften, expand, and move beyond personal preference.

### 3. Compassion (*Karunā*) – The Wish to Alleviate Suffering

Compassion (*karuna*), or the heartfelt wish for suffering to be alleviated, arises when we fully open to the reality of others' pain. It is not a passive feeling of sorrow but an active response that moves us beyond indifference and into engagement.

True compassion is not feeling bad for others as if they are separate. True compassion is a way of truly being with those who suffer. This may take the form of direct help, offering material or emotional support, or standing up against injustice. At other times, it is expressed through presence or listening deeply, holding space, and providing comfort. Even when we cannot physically intervene, compassion remains boundless, flowing through prayers, good wishes, and an unwavering intention for others' well-being. In this way, compassion is not just an emotion but a living expression of ethical conduct, guiding us toward skillful, caring engagement with the world.

## The Near and Far Enemies of Compassion

- **Far Enemy: Cruelty**—The wish to inflict suffering, or indifference to the suffering of others.

- **Near Enemy: Pity**—A subtle feeling of superiority, seeing others as "below" us, feeling separate and "sorry" for others rather than connected.

Compassion does not mean taking on the suffering of others in a way that is personally harmful. Instead, it means meeting suffering with deep connection and responding in ways that are helpful rather than over-whelming.

## Self-Compassion

One of the most overlooked aspects of compassion, especially in spiritual communities, is self-compassion. Many practitioners are taught to extend care to others while unknowingly or unintentionally neglecting them-selves, believing that self-directed care is selfish or indul-gent. However, true compassion must include oneself, recognizing that we, too, are sentient beings worthy of care. Without self-compassion, our capacity to serve oth-ers is limited, often leading to burnout, resentment, or spiritual bypassing. By treating our own relative suffering with the same tenderness we offer to others, we cultivate resilience, deepen our practice, and model the kind of balanced compassion we hope to see in the world.

## Practicing Compassion

A powerful method to cultivate compassion is *Ton-glen* (Sending and Receiving Meditation):

1. **Diamond:** Imagine that you have a magical diamond in your heart that can transform

suffering into healing compassion.

2. **Inhale:** Breathing in the suffering of a loved one. Take it into the diamond in your heart, transforming it into light.

3. **Exhale:** Send them relief, healing, and compassion. Imagine suffering dissolving into a boundless field of care.

4. **Expand:** Extend this practice to all beings in pain.

This practice reverses self-centeredness, helping us open to suffering without fear or avoidance. *If you struggle with self-compassion, try doing this practice for yourself while looking into a mirror.* Breathing in your own suffering and exhaling compassion to your reflection.

## 4. Sympathetic Joy (*Muditā*) – Taking Joy in the Joy of Others

Sympathetic joy (*Mudita*) is the practice of rejoicing in the happiness and success of others. It is the opposite of envy and comparison.

- When someone else succeeds, we often feel envy (Why not me?).

- When others are happy, we may feel resentment (*They don't deserve it!*).

*Mudita* shifts us from scarcity to abundance, helping us see that joy is not a limited resource.

### The Near and Far Enemies of Sympathetic Joy

- **Far Enemy: envy**—Feeling bitter about others' happiness or success.

- **Near Enemy: self-centered joy**—Being excited for someone else based on what you would want, not on what they would want (e.g, imagine receiving a gift that was more about the gift giver's excitement than it was about your own excitement).

## Practicing Sympathetic Joy

- When someone succeeds, silently affirm: *"May your happiness continue."*
- Reflect: *"Another's happiness does not diminish my own."*
- Extend this joy not just to loved ones, but even to strangers and difficult people.

Sympathetic Joy helps dissolve comparison, competition, and the fear of not being enough. It allows us to see others' joy as our own joy.

## Closing Reflection: Cultivating a Boundless Heart

So I invite you to reflect:

- Where in your life are you holding back love?
- Do you only wish happiness for those you like?
- How would your life change if you extended love even to those you struggle with?

## Bridging into Bodhicitta

These Four Immeasurables are the foundation for the next step: *Bodhicitta*. Once we have trained the heart to be vast and open, we can commit to Awakening not just for ourselves, but for all beings.

For now, simply remember:

*A liberated heart is vast, all-embracing, and boundlessly open, radiating unconditional love, compassion, joy, and to all beings impartially.*

## Chapter 10

# BODHICITTA

## Awakening for the Benefit of All Beings

In the previous chapter, we explored The Four Immeasurables of equanimity, unconditional love, compassion, and sympathetic joy. These boundless qualities expand our hearts and dissolve the illusion of separateness, allowing us to relate to all beings with openness and care.

But The Four Immeasurables are not the end of the path. The Four Immeasurables serve as building blocks for an even greater shift to a radical transformation of the heart known as Bodhicitta.

Bodhicitta is the deep wish to awaken, not just for our own benefit, but for the liberation and benefit of all beings.

Bodhicitta is the force that propels the Bodhisattva Vow. The Bodhisattva Vow is the commitment to attain enlightenment for the benefit of all sentient beings. This vow is made by those who dedicate their lives to wisdom, compassion, and Awakening.

Without bodhicitta, wisdom remains dry meaning that it may reveal profound truths, but it lacks warmth, responsiveness, and embodied love. With bodhicitta, wisdom is fully alive, radiating as compassion in every action, word, and thought dedicated to the benefit of each and every being.

This is what makes the Bodhisattva ideal unique. Unlike other paths that focus on personal enlightenment, the Bodhisattva does not seek to simply escape suffering. Instead, they find liberation from suffering and at the same time remain engaged with the world, turning their Awakening toward the well-being of others.

**The Three Aspects of Bodhicitta**

Bodhicitta, the awakened heart-mind, has both relative and ultimate dimensions. The relative dimension can be further divided into aspirational and engaged aspects. Together, these three dimensions form a complete expression bodhicitta.

- **Relative Bodhicitta**

  ◊ **Aspirational**—The Vow to Liberate All Beings – The heartfelt wish for all beings to be free from suffering and attain Awakening. It is the deep aspiration to cultivate equanimity, love, compassion, and joy for the benefit of others, even before one has the full capacity to act on it.

  ◊ **Engaged Bodhicitta**—Compassion in Action – The active, embodied commitment to serve and benefit others. This includes practicing the Six Perfections discussed in the next chapter.

  ◊ **Ultimate Bodhicitta**—Living from the Recognition of Awakening – The direct, embodied realization that samsara and nirvana are not two, and that Awakening is already present. This manifests as spontaneous, effortless compassion and wisdom, guiding beings without attachment to outcomes or conceptual striving. One aspect of this ultimate bodhicitta is the recognition that although there are no "others" compassion to alleviate suffering is endless.

Bodhicitta requires both aspiration (the heartfelt wish) and engagement (the lived expression). Together, along with ultimate bodhicitta, these form the complete path of the bodhisattva, balancing compassionate action with deep wisdom.

The simultaneous reality of both relative and ultimate bodhicitta is the great paradox of the Bodhisattva. A bodhisattva dedicates their life to freeing beings from suffering, yet they also see that there is no ultimate separation."

As my mentor, Ken Wilber, often says in regard to the Bodhisattva Vow, "There are no others, therefore I vow to liberate them all."

## The Natural Evolution of Bodhicitta in Practice

Bodhicitta does not arise all at once but rather it unfolds through a gradual expansion of the heart. There are several key stages in its development and practice:

### 1. Recognizing That All Beings Seek Happiness

At first, we feel as if our suffering is uniquely ours, but through meditation and reflection, we begin to see that all beings, without exception, long for happiness and wish to avoid suffering. The desire to be loved, safe, and free from suffering is universal since it transcends species, cultures, and lifetimes. Even those who cause harm are acting from a confused attempt to find happiness, though they may seek it in harmful ways. Every being, no matter how they appear, is just like us for everybody is seeking peace, security, and fulfillment.

When this realization moves from an idea to a direct experience, something shifts. The heart naturally opens, and we begin to see others not as obstacles or threats, but as fellow travelers on the path.

## 2. The Birth of the Bodhisattva Aspiration

At a certain point, something profound shifts. We no longer seek Awakening solely for our own peace and freedom, nor do we limit our wish for enlightenment to only those we feel close to. Instead, we come to see that our liberation is inseparable from the liberation of all beings. From this realization, a deep wish arises: May I awaken, not for myself alone, but to serve and uplift all beings. This is the birth of bodhicitta.

It is not an abstract wish but it is a commitment to the Bodhisattva path, a lifelong dedication to Awakening for the benefit of others. For some, this aspiration may arise after some specific event opens their heart. For others, the aspiration arises in a gradual way through practice. And there are some for whom bodhicitta doesn't arise in a full and authentic way until after their first taste of Awakening. Once a person knows that true liberation is possible, one of the most natural expressions is to want that same freedom for others.

## 3. A Practice to Expand the Circle of Bodhicitta

In one of the practices described in the last chapter on loving-kindness, we expanded our heart by gradually extending care from those we feel close to, to neutral individuals, and finally to those we find difficult. We can apply the same approach to cultivating bodhicitta. The key difference here is that our aspiration now goes beyond simply wishing others well. Now, with a heart full of bodhicitta, we focus on Awakening. We wish for all others to realize total and complete enlightenment.

- **Begin with loved ones** – Generate the sincere wish for those closest to you to attain total and complete enlightenment.

- **Expand to neutral people** – Extend the same aspiration to those you usually overlook or feel indifferent toward.

- **Include difficult individuals** – Open your heart to even those who have harmed or challenged you, wishing for their Awakening.

- **Hold all beings equally** – Gradually dissolve boundaries, embracing all sentient beings with the same unwavering aspiration for their total and complete enlightenment.

This does not mean we force ourselves to feel love for everyone instantly. It is a gradual training of the heart, supported by practice and our ever-deepening realization.

## Bodhicitta as the Natural Expression of Wisdom

At the highest level, bodhicitta is not separate from wisdom. From the perspective of emptiness (*shunyata*), all beings are already interconnected and free although they do not realize it. A Bodhisattva sees both the suffering of beings and their true nature simultaneously.

This is why bodhicitta is not about fixing others but is about helping them recognize the freedom that is already present within them.

This is the union of relative and ultimate bodhicitta:

- **Relative bodhicitta** moves us to act, to serve, and to uplift others.

- **Ultimate bodhicitta** reminds us that Awakening is already present in us and all beings, it only needs to be revealed.

A true Bodhisattva walks the path joyfully, without heaviness or self-sacrifice. The Bodhisattva does not save others; they simply help them see what has been there all along.

## Closing Reflection: Cultivating Bodhicitta in Daily Life

Bodhicitta is something we cultivate in the small moments of daily life, not just something we merely aspire to.

So I invite you to reflect:

- Who in your life do you truly wish finds full and complete enlightenment? Who do you struggle to include?

- How would your life change if you saw no separation between your enlightenment and the enlightenment of others?

- What small action can you take today to uplift someone else and inspire them in the path of Awakening?

In the next chapter, we will explore The Six Perfections or the six practices that bring bodhicitta into action, transforming the bodhisattva intention into a lived reality.

For now, simply remember:

*Bodhicitta is the bridge between wisdom and love—it is the heart of Awakening for the benefit of all beings.*

Chapter 11

# THE SIX PERFECTIONS

## Bringing Wisdom and Compassion into Action

In the previous chapter, we explored bodhicitta, which is the deep aspiration to awaken, not just for our own liberation, but for the benefit and Awakening of all beings. However, bodhicitta is not just a mental or emotional state but must be expressed through lived action.

The last two chapters have already started to introduce the movement from intention to action. Practices related to the Four Immeasurables showed us how to bring the aspirational bodhicitta of a boundless heart into lived experience. The practice described in the last chapter, expanding the circle of bodhicitta, translated the aspiration for Awakening into our direct relationships.

This chapter takes it even further. The Six Perfections provide a structured framework for how a Bodhisattva brings Awakening into the world through action. This is engaged bodhicitta. These perfections are the true expression of an open, awakened heart.

### The Six Perfections (*Paramitas*)

The Six Perfections (*Paramitas*) form the heart of the bodhisattva's path, seamlessly interwoven as a continuous unfolding of wisdom and compassion. The Six Perfections are:

1. **Generosity (*Dana*)** – The practice of giving without attachment.

2. **Ethical Conduct (*Shila*)** – Living in alignment with wisdom and non-harm.

3. **Patience (*Kshanti*)** – Meeting difficulties with stability and compassion.

4. **Joyful Effort (*Virya*)** – Enthusiastic perseverance on the path.

5. **Concentration (*Dhyana*)** – Cultivating clarity, stillness, and focused attention.

6. **Wisdom (*Prajna*)** – Seeing through illusion and realizing the true nature of reality.

Each perfection arises naturally from the previous one, forming an integrated and progressive path toward Awakening.

**Generosity** (*Dana*) arises organically from sympathetic joy and bodhicitta. When we rejoice in the happiness of others, selfless giving flows effortlessly. Similarly, as we cultivate bodhicitta, or the heartfelt wish for all beings to benefit, generosity becomes an instinctive expression of that awakened intention.

**Ethical conduct** (*Shila*) builds upon generosity. As we give to others, we begin to cultivate a natural sense of fairness, integrity, and considerateness. This ethical foundation sustains and deepens our capacity to benefit others and accumulate positive merit, creating the conditions for a trustworthy and wholesome life.

**Patience** (*Kshanti*) serves to protect the merit and positivity developed through ethical living. Anger and reactivity can quickly erode the positive energy we have generated; patience stabilizes and preserves it, allowing us to respond with clarity and care even in challenging situations.

**Joyful effort** (*Virya*) is rooted in patience. With a steady and calm mind, perseverance arises naturally. Instead of pushing or straining, our energy becomes steady and resilient, allowing us to engage with the path wholeheartedly and without burnout.

**Concentration** (*Dhyana*) is sustained by this joyful effort. As energy becomes stable and focused, deep meditation becomes possible. Without the fuel of effort, the mind easily wanders; with it, concentration deepens, bringing calm and clarity.

**Wisdom** (*Prajna*) arises from the stillness and clarity of concentration. With a mind that is no longer agitated or distracted, we can directly investigate the nature of reality. Insight into emptiness and the true nondual nature of experience emerges, revealing the essence of Awakening.

By practicing all six perfections, we develop a complete and balanced path of Awakening, one that harmonizes compassion, ethical conduct, meditative stability, and profound insight.

## Three Levels and Near and Far Enemies of the Six Perfections

Each of the perfections can be understood at three levels:

1. **The Conventional Level** – Ordinary expressions of generosity, patience, ethical behavior, etc.

2. **The Deeper Level** – Practicing these qualities with increasing wisdom and non-attachment.

3. **The Highest Level** – Seeing each practice through the lens of emptiness and nonduality, where the three spheres of subject, object, and act of expressing the perfection itself dissolve into spontaneous, selfless activity.

In addition to these three levels of understanding, like all virtues, each of the Six Perfections (paramitas) has both near enemies, or qualities that appear similar yet ultimately miss the mark, and far enemies, which are their direct opposites. Recognizing these distinctions refines our practice, allowing the perfections to mature from conventional goodness into fully awakened activity.

We explore the near and far enemies and the three levels of expression below.

### 1. Generosity (*Dana*): Giving without Attachment

At the conventional level, generosity means offering resources, time, or kindness to others. At a deeper level, it arises from bodhicitta or the awakened heart that seeks to give freely without self-reference. At the highest level, generosity is no longer about "me" giving to "you" but rather becomes an effortless flow infused with nondual awareness.

As the Diamond Sutra teaches: *"A Bodhisattva should give without perceiving a giver, a gift, or a receiver. Only then is it true giving."*

This is nondual generosity, the highest form of giving, free from attachment, flowing spontaneously like space into space.

## Near and Far Enemies of Generosity

- **Far Enemy:** Greed, stinginess, selfishness.
- **Near Enemy:** Conditional giving or giving with the expectation of return, recognition, or control.

## A Practice to Increase Generosity

### Daily Act of Giving

Choose one small, intentional act of generosity each day, whether offering your time, a kind word, or a material gift. Before the act, pause and reflect: May this offering benefit others without expectation or attachment. Over time, this practice loosens clinging, opens the heart, and transforms everyday moments into expressions of selfless giving.

## 2. Ethical Conduct (*Shila*): The Path of Positive Conduct and Virtue

At the conventional level, ethics means following moral guidelines, avoiding harm, and cultivating virtue. At the deeper level, morality arises from a deep understanding of our interconnectedness rather than a fixed sense of rules. At the highest level, ethical conduct is about naturally aligning our actions with reality itself. At this level of expression self, other, and activity dissolve into the single awakened action.

## Near and Far Enemies of Ethical Conduct

- **Far Enemy:** Immorality, deceit, manipulation, harm to others.

- **Near Enemy:** Rigid morality or an ethical conduct based on self-righteousness, judgment, or rigid attachment to rules rather than wisdom.

## A Practice to Increase Ethical Conduct

### Mindful Review of Speech and Action

At the end of each day, take a few quiet moments to reflect: Were my actions rooted in kindness, honesty, and respect? Did I cause harm or speak unskillfully? Without judgment or self-criticism, gently recommit to living in greater alignment. This daily review strengthens integrity and supports the cultivation of a life guided by ethical presence.

### 3. Patience (*Kshanti*): Protecting the Merit and Stability of the Mind

At the conventional level, patience is like a shield that protects us from creativity and angry outbursts which can erode our positive karma and merit. At the deeper level, patience becomes an active practice of maintaining inner stability and meditative presence despite external chaos. At the highest level, patience is the recognition that there is no separate self to be harmed and no independent entities causing harm. All events arising in our environment are teachers, inviting us into deeper compassion and understanding. As one text says, "if we could see any situation fully, the only appropriate response would be compassion."

In his classic work, *The Way of the Bodhisattva*, Shantideva says:

*"If something can be remedied, why be upset about it? If there is no remedy, what is the use of being upset?"*

In addition to Shantideva's practical advice we can also use the lens of emptiness. Through emptiness, we inquire: *Who is angry? Who is harmed? Where is this "I" that needs defending?*

By looking closely into the nature of both the self and the phenomena in any given situation, anger dissolves, revealing a spacious, compassionate presence.

### Near and Far Enemies of Patience

- **Far Enemy:** Anger, impatience, frustration.

- **Near Enemy:** Complacency or a passivity that tolerates injustice or harm rather than engaging with wisdom.

### A Practice to Increase Patience

### The Three-Breath Pause

When irritation or discomfort arises, practice pausing for three full breaths before reacting. Feel the sensations in your body and observe the urge to speak or act. In this small space, choose steadiness over reactivity. By returning to patience again and again, you build the capacity to remain open-hearted, even in challenging situations.

### 4. Joyful Effort (*Virya*): The Energy That Sustains the Path

At the conventional level, effort means working hard toward spiritual practice. At the deeper level, it transforms into delight in the path itself, a natural enthusiasm for Awakening. At the highest level, effort dissolves into inexhaustible, effortless action.

Through recognizing emptiness, we see that there is no meditator, no effort, and no goal but is just the natural play of awareness. This is how, as the practice deepens, joyful effort self-liberates into spontaneous presence.

### Near and Far Enemies of Joyful Effort

- **Far Enemy:** Procrastination and apathy.

- **Near Enemy:** Overexertion, self-punishment, and perfectionism. These tendencies can be a way of pushing oneself that leads to burnout rather than sustainable, enthusiastic perseverance.

## A Practice to Increase Joyful Effort

### Setting Daily Intentions with Inspiration

Each morning, reconnect with your deepest purpose. Say silently: May I use this day to benefit others and grow on the path. Let this intention lift your heart and energize your actions. Joyful effort arises from remembering what truly matters and moving toward it with enthusiasm.

### 5. Concentration (*Dhyana*): Deepening Focus and Clarity

At the conventional level, meditation is about concentration and calming the mind. At the deeper level, concentration provides a foundation for insight. At the highest level, concentration meditation stabilizes the view of Awakened Awareness in all times and all situations. This highest level represents the union of concentration and insight.

### Near and Far Enemies of Meditation

- **Far Enemy:** Distraction, dullness, restlessness.
- **Near Enemy:** Tranquilization, escape. This occurs when a practitioner uses concentration meditation to avoid life rather than a means to insight.

## A Practice to Increase Concentration

### Single-Object Meditation

Set aside 10 to 15 minutes and rest your attention on a single object, such as your breath, your body, a mantra, or a visual image. When the mind wanders, return to the object of focus. This steady returning builds attentional strength and quiets the restless tendencies of the mind, allowing deeper stillness and focus to emerge. (We discuss a detailed overview of concentration in the next chapter.)

## 6. Wisdom (*Prajna*): The Culmination of the Path

At the conventional level, wisdom means learning about the nature of reality. At the deeper level, it involves direct insight into emptiness. At the highest level, wisdom transcends even the idea of a "path" or "attainment" and relates to directly knowing one's true nature as fully Enlightened Awareness.

### Near and Far Enemies of Wisdom

- **Far Enemy:** Ignorance, confusion, delusion.
- **Near Enemy:** False wisdom, conceptualization. This occurs when one confuses an intellectual understanding of emptiness with direct realization.

### A Practice to Increase Wisdom

### Contemplative Inquiry into Emptiness

After you've calmed the mind through a period of concentration meditation, gently inquire into the nature of your experience. Ask: Where is the solid self? Can I find the self anywhere in the body or the mental content? What is the true nature of this thought or emotion? Does it have any substance, shape, or color? Allow insights into impermanence, interdependence, and emptiness to arise naturally. Over time, this practice unveils the deeper truth of reality and the nature of awareness. (We discuss a detailed overview of wisdom and this kind of insight meditation in the Chapter 13.)

## Closing Reflection: Integrating the Perfections into Daily Life

Use the outlines of the Six Perfections above to shape your own understanding and guide your practice. As you integrate them into daily life, notice how each perfection builds upon the others, weaving together a full and balanced path of Awakening.

In particular, keep an eye out for the near enemies of each perfection or those subtle distortions that masquerade as the real thing. Conditional giving may look like generosity but hides expectation. Rigid morality can feel like ethics but conceals judgment. Complacency may pass as patience but it lacks responsiveness. Overexertion mimics joyful effort but leads to burnout. Escaping into stillness appears to be concentration but can be a way of avoiding life. Intellectualizing insight seems like wisdom but without direct experience is not genuine.

Practitioners can spend many years "missing the mark" even with sincere intentions. By staying attuned to these subtle traps, you refine your discernment and allow each perfection to express itself with increasing authenticity, depth, and freedom.

Here are a few contemplations for you to consider:

- Which of the near enemies do you need to be more aware of in your own life?

- How does your understanding of emptiness and nonduality change your practice of generosity, ethics, and patience?

- Where do you experience resistance or imbalance in the Six Perfections?

- What would it mean to practice these perfections without a sense of self "doing" them?

In the next chapter, we explore concentration meditation, the fifth perfection, in detail.

For now, simply remember:

*The Six Perfections provide a structured path for a bodhisattva to bring their Awakening into the world.*

# Chapter 12

# CONCENTRATION MEDITATION

## Taming the Min

In the previous chapter, we explored the Six Perfections (Paramitas) or the six qualities that transform bodhicitta into lived action. Each perfection refines the mind, dissolving self-centeredness and strengthening our ability to walk the path of the bodhisattva.

Among the Six Perfections, the fifth perfection—meditative concentration (*Dhyana*)—stands out as a pivotal factor for deeper realization. Generosity, ethical conduct, patience, and joyful effort set the stage for transformation, but without the ability to focus and stabilize the mind, wisdom remains superficial.

It is at this stage in the path when developing a meditation practice becomes absolutely essential.

## The Two Core Types of Meditation

Buddhist meditation consists of two primary dimensions, which together form a complete path of transformation:

### 1. Concentration Meditation (*śamatha*)

◊ The practice of cultivating inner stillness by training the mind to rest on a single object, such as the breath, the body, a mantra, or an image.

◊ This kind of meditation develops focused attention, clarity, and tranquility, providing a foundation for insight.

◊ This is the focus of the 5th perfection.

## 2. **Insight Meditation** (*vipaśyanā*)

◊ The practice of investigating the nature of experience, seeing through illusions of permanence, self, and solidity.

◊ Insight reveals that all experiences arise and dissolve, leading to direct recognition of impermanence, emptiness, and interdependence.

◊ This is the cultivation of wisdom and is the focus of the 6th perfection.

Both of these types of meditation are necessary. Without concentration, insight is unstable. Without insight, concentration does not lead to true freedom. Together, they lead to deep stable transformation resulting in the recognition of Awakened Awareness.

We focus on concentration meditation here in this chapter. We discuss insight meditation and wisdom in the next chapter.

## The Problem of the Untrained Mind

Imagine trying to see the reflection of the moon in a pond. If the water is agitated and murky, the reflection will be distorted. But if the water becomes still and clear, the moon is perfectly reflected with clarity and precision. Our minds function in the same way. When we are caught in distraction, craving, anxiety, and reactivity, we cannot see things clearly. But when the mind is settled, stable, and aware, we can begin to perceive reality as it is.

The Buddha said that the untrained mind is like a wild elephant, thrashing through a village. It is destruc-

tive, restless, and difficult to control. Without practice, our minds are driven by habits, impulses, and emotional reactions, leading to unnecessary suffering.

Concentration meditation is the method of how to train the wild elephant of the mind. Through concentration, the wild elephant of the mind is made calm. Through concentration practice, we learn to guide the mind toward steadiness, focus, and clarity.

## Training the Wild Elephant

Concentration Meditation (*shamatha*) is the art of training the mind. We learn to transform our habitual state of scatteredness and distraction into stability and clarity.

Yet, training the mind is not always easy. At first, the mind resists stillness, distracted by thoughts, physical discomfort, and external stimuli. Like an untamed elephant that thrashes against its restraints, the mind struggles when we try to get it to focus on a single object. It seeks escape and distraction in memories, worries, or fantasies. This is normal. The key is persistence and a clear method for guiding the mind step by step toward deeper concentration.

To understand the process of training the mind, we turn to Asanga's Nine Stages of Concentration. Asanga's stages of concentration originated in 506 CE. It is a time-tested roadmap for refining our capacity to sustain attention.

## The Nine Stages of Concentration: The Elephant Path

The journey of training the mind is traditionally illustrated by the Elephant Path thangka (see image). This thangka is an ancient Tibetan painting that depicts a meditator and an elephant along a winding road. There are nine elephants moving vertically along the path. Each elephant, representing the mind itself, symbolizes a new stage of concentration. The elephant begins wild and dark, symbolizing distraction and dullness.

At the beginning of the path (bottom right) the meditator is holding two tools, the *rope of mindfulness* and the *hook of knowing*. The rope of mindfulness represents our capacity to tie our mind to a meditation object. The hook of knowing represents our capacity to monitor our experience and to detect distraction.

As training progresses, the elephant becomes calmer, eventually turning white, symbolizing purified awareness. The monkey, representing distraction, eventually disappears, while the meditator gains mastery over the elephant by walking confidently and effortlessly, no longer needing a rope or a hook.

Each of the Nine Stages of Concentration describes a distinct level of mental development, from complete restlessness to unwavering stability. Understanding this map allows us to navigate our own meditation practice with patience and precision.

## <u>STAGE 1</u>: Settling the Mind (Scattered Attention)

### Taming the Elephant Begins — The Mind is Like a Rushing, Turbulent Waterfall

The practice begins with setting the proper body posture and selecting a single object of focus. The object of focus can be the breath, sensations in the body, a mantra, or a visualization.

At this initial stage of meditation, the mind is completely unsettled, leaping chaotically from one thought to the next. Like a wild elephant, it is out of control and easily drawn away by sensory experiences and mental distractions. The meditator, in response, is equipped with two essential tools: the rope of mindfulness and the hook of knowing. The rope of mindfulness symbolizes our ability to tether the mind to the chosen object of meditation, while the hook of knowing represents the inner faculty that monitors our experience and detects when the mind has drifted.

The core task at this stage is to continually re-tie the rope of mindfulness to the object of focus each time it wanders. This process must be repeated again and again throughout the session. During this early phase, *periods of distraction typically far outnumber moments of sustained attention*. This stage is the most difficult part of the training. It requires a kind of forcible engagement by learning simply to sit still and begin cultivating the most fundamental level of concentration.

## STAGE 2: Continuous Settling (Developing Sustained Attention)

### Extending the Flow of Concentration

In this second stage, the meditator begins to engage a third tool: the flames of curiosity. Alongside the rope of mindfulness and the hook of knowing, curiosity adds interest to the practice. As interest in the meditation object increases, attention naturally stays focused for longer stretches.

Distractions still arise, but attention is more stable and less easily pulled away. The meditator begins to develop the strength to hold continuous attention on the meditation object. At this stage, periods of sustained focus begin to outlast periods of distraction.

The key practice at this stage is to intentionally increase your curiosity and interest in the meditation object. This is called tightening the rope of mindfulness. At this stage you learn to be more interested in the object than you are in the distractions. When the mind wanders, return to the object and tighten the rope a bit more, increasing intimacy with the object.

## STAGE 3: Resettling (Recognizing Distraction Quickly and Redirecting Awareness)

## Sharpening the hook — Redirecting the Elephant back on Track

In the third stage, distraction still occurs, but the meditator now recognizes it much more quickly. Instead of being carried away for long stretches, attention returns to the object almost immediately. This growing sensitivity marks a key turning point: the ability to notice mind-wandering before it gains momentum.

The task is no longer just to return to the object, but to catch distraction in its earliest stages, that is, to notice the very moment attention begins to drift. With this sharpened hook of knowing, stability increases and continuity of attention strengthens.

The key practice is to continue deepening curiosity and interest in the meditation object. Let that engagement anchor attention more naturally. At the same time, strengthen the habit of returning immediately without indulging in or analyzing distractions. Each quick return reinforces the pattern of presence.

## <u>STAGE 4</u>: Complete Settling (Refining Vigilance and Balancing Energy)

### The Mind is Like the Continuous Flow of a River

In the fourth stage, concentration has noticeably improved, but a new challenge emerges: balancing the mind's energy. Some meditators begin to apply too much effort, gripping the meditation object with intensity and becoming agitated. Others relax too much, slipping into dullness or lethargy. Both extremes interfere with stable attention.

This is the stage where meditation becomes a refined skill, requiring sensitivity and precision. It's like tuning a stringed instrument where the mind must be not too tight and not too loose. The right balance allows attention to rest with clarity and stability.

The key practice here is to find a calm yet alert state,

free from both agitation and dullness. Use the specific methods your teacher provides to balance your inner energy.

At this stage you may notice stretches of not just *continuous* focus over time, but also glimpses of *complete* focus at any given moment in time. For example, even if the meditator achieves relatively continuous focus, the strength of that focus can be either partial or complete. Partial focus is when attention is relatively continuous on the meditation object overtime but divided at any given moment in time. In other words, part of the attention is on the meditation object and while another part is paying attention to the inner meditation coach guiding the practice or wandering in distraction. Alternatively, complete focus is when attention is relatively continuous on the meditation object overtime and simultaneously it is fully immersed in the object at any given moment in time. In complete focus, attention is not divided. Even the inner meditation coach is made calm.

## STAGE 5: Taming (Recognizing the Benefits and Refining Perception)

### Through Increased Curiosity the Meditator Opens More Subtle Levels of Perception

In the fifth stage, the mind begins to feel at home in stable concentration. Meditation is no longer something you have to push through; instead, there's a natural enjoyment of the meditative state that concentration brings. Attention settles more easily, and the inner environment feels calm, open, and clear.

Through increased curiosity, subtle perception begins to emerge. Fine details of the meditation object become more vivid. The object that once seemed solid, now feels more fluid and insubstantial. This subtle perception reveals layers of experience that were previously obscured by dividing attention.

The key practice at this stage is to develop even deeper interest and curiosity about the object. As curiosity deepens, the object begins to reveal its impermanent and insubstantial nature.

## STAGE 6: Pacifying (Loosening the Rope and Glimpsing Effortlessness)

### The Elephant Walks Calmly — Meditation Becomes Easy

In the sixth stage, effort begins to dissolve. Instead of holding attention through deliberate engagement, focus starts to feel light, natural, and effortless. The mind stays with the object on its own, without strain. A subtle joy begins to arise, one that comes from simply being present.

At this stage, some meditators may begin to glimpse states of deep ease, where the practice seems to carry itself. This marks a quiet turning point: concentration no longer feels like something you're doing, but something you're allowing.

The key practice here is to loosen the rope of mindfulness just enough to let attention rest without losing the thread of continuity. Allow the practice to begin maintaining itself by itself.

## STAGE 7: Complete Pacifying (Letting Go of Attachment to Samadhi)

### Moving Beyond Effort in a Stable Way

In the seventh stage, effortlessness becomes stable. At this stage, concentration unfolds naturally, without force, and attention is smooth and even. There is a growing trust in the mind's natural stability.

Rather than managing or correcting the practice, the meditator now rests in a quiet confidence allowing the process to unfold on its own. Awareness remains present without needing to be held.

The key practice is to loosen the rope even more to discover stability, even effortlessness. The elephant is completely pacified.

## STAGE 8: One-Pointedness (Unshakable Concentration)

### The Elephant Now Follows Without Resistance

In the eighth stage, attention is so stable that nothing more than the slightest intention to meditate is enough since the mind follows instantly. Distractions no longer arise as intrusions; if they appear at all, they dissolve upon arising, leaving awareness undisturbed.

At this stage the meditator makes very fine adjustments to tightening and loosening.

The key practice is to simply rest completely into the object while learning to make subtle refinements. Slightly tightening or loosening brings the meditation object into optimal vividness and one-pointed clarity.

## STAGE 9: Tranquility / Equanimity (Perfect Concentration)

### The Elephant is Fully Trained; The Mind is like a Vast Still Ocean

In the ninth stage, distraction has completely subsided. The mind remains effortlessly stable, regardless of circumstances. Concentration is no longer confined to formal meditation, whether sitting, walking, eating, or speaking, the same unwavering presence is available. Attention is fully integrated into daily life, and awareness remains bright, centered, and undisturbed.

This level of training represents a culmination of concentration practice and serves as the ideal foundation for deeper insight work, including advanced paths like Mahamudra and Dzogchen, where stability of mind is essential for recognizing the nature of awareness.

The key practice at this final stage is to lock in to perfect concentration. Because concentration is a transferable skill, the practitioner has the capacity to move through the world with the same stable, laser-focused presence that was cultivated on the cushion.

## The Fruits of a Tamed Mind

As meditation deepens, the wild elephant of the mind becomes an ally rather than an enemy. Instead of being dragged about by distractions and impulses, we learn to move through life with clarity, presence, and ease. The once-chaotic mind now serves the path of wisdom. In this way, the tradition says that at the later stages of concentration the mind is fully "serviceable."

Concentration meditation is a journey that can require commitment, but with each step, the mind becomes more stable and calm.

## Closing Reflection: Where Are You on the Path of Concentration?

- Which stage best describes your current concentration meditation practice?

- Where do you struggle most: distraction, dullness, efforting?

- What would it feel like to meditate with complete ease?

In the next chapter, we will explore how deep concentration leads to liberating wisdom.

For now, simply remember:

*A well trained mind is the basis for the cultivation of insight into your true nature.*

Chapter 13

# INSIGHT MEDITATION

## Seeing Through Relative Experience and Recognizing Our True Nature

In the previous chapter, we explored concentration meditation as the way to train inner stability and presence. But meditation is not just about calming the mind but is about seeing reality clearly without obscurations.

As the mind settles, we have an opportunity to look directly into the nature of the mind itself and recognize the habitual distortions that shape our experience. The practice that supports this is called Insight Meditation.

Insight meditation (*Vipaśyanā*) is the practice of seeing through the layers of obscuration that cloud our direct experience of reality. Insight Meditation, also called *lak-tong in Tibetan,* translates directly as "clear-seeing." In this practice, one cuts through illusion, revealing the mind's innate clarity and emptiness. By penetrating the veils of habitual perception, this practice unveils the true nature of awareness where all phenomena arise and dissolve within the vast, luminous openness of awareness itself. This is wisdom, the Sixth Perfection.

## The Three Turnings of the Wheel of Dharma

To help us see through these obscurations, the Buddha taught the Dharma in three great phases, known as the Three Turnings of the Wheel of Dharma. Each Turning reveals a deeper level of insight or truth:

1. **The First Turning:** The Three Marks of Existence – Reveals the impermanent, unsatisfactory, and selfless nature of all conditioned experience.

2. **The Second Turning: Emptiness and Interdependence** – One sees through the illusion of inherent, independently existing entities (Skt. śūnyatā) and realizes the interdependent nature of all things. This naturally awakens the heart to compassion.

3. **The Third Turning:** Buddha-Nature – The meditator recognizes that Awakening is already present within us. Our true nature and the true nature of all beings is already awake and free.

These three phases of Buddhist teachings each offer a new level of insight. We explore each of them below in greater detail.

## The First Turning: The Three Marks of Existence

The First Turning of the Wheel took place when the Buddha gave his first teaching at Deer Park in Sarnath. Here, he laid out the basic structure of conditioned existence, explaining why suffering arises and how we can move beyond it.

The foundation of this teaching is the Three Marks of Existence:

1. **Impermanence** (Skt. *anitya*) – Everything is constantly changing.

2. **Suffering** (Skt. *duḥkha*) – We cling to what is

impermanent, we experience dissatisfaction.

3. **Non-Self** (Skt. *anātman*) – There is no solid, fixed self but only a dynamic unfolding of experience.

Let's look at each of the Three Marks one by one.

## 1. Impermanence – Nothing Stays the Same

Everything changes, including our bodies, emotions, relationships, and even thoughts exist in a state of constant flux. All phenomena are endlessly arising and dissolving. Suffering arises when we resist this truth, clinging to what is fleeting and attempting to hold onto that which is inherently transitory. Yet, as we explored in Chapter 4, impermanence is not merely something to fear but is the very condition that allows for growth, transformation, and Awakening. Without change, there would be no possibility of liberation; it is through embracing impermanence that we find the gateway to true freedom.

## 2. Suffering – The Unreliability of Conditioned Existence

*Dukkha* is not just suffering but is the inherent instability and unreliability of conditioned existence.

We experience many faces of suffering:

- **Pain and loss** – The suffering of suffering (*dukkha-dukkha*).

- **Anxiety over change** – The suffering of change (*viparinama-dukkha*).

- **Subtle dissatisfaction** – The suffering of conditioned existence (*sankhara-dukkha*).

Recognizing this truth is not pessimism. Instead it serves as the gateway to freedom. As we explored in Chapter 6, understanding the nature of suffering is an important step toward liberation.

### 3. Non-Self – The Illusion of a Separate "I"

One of the most radical teachings of the First Turning is *Anatta* (Non-Self).

We tend to think of the self as a thing, as a solid, enduring identity.

But the Buddha taught that the self is not a fixed entity but is a process, a constantly shifting interplay of thoughts, emotions, perceptions, and memories.

If we look closely, we find that the self is not something we "are" but is something we "do." *The self is more like a verb rather than a noun.* We are "selfing" more than we are an actual independently existing, solid "self."

## The Second Turning:
## Emptiness and Interdependence

The Second Turning goes deeper. It introduces the notion of emptiness and interdependence.

Emptiness moves beyond the notion of impermanence and "non-self" to bring into question whether anything at all has inherent, independent existence.

There are two aspects to emptiness practice:

(1) Emptiness of Self and

(2) Emptiness of Phenomena(

In the Tibetan teachings, these emptiness practices are at the very heart of Insight Meditation.

### 1. The Emptiness of Self – Like a Rainbow in the Sky

To better understand the emptiness of self, consider the nature of a rainbow. A rainbow appears vivid and real, yet it has no solid substance. It arises only when the right causes and conditions—sunlight, moisture, and perspective—come together. Though it appears before us, there is no fixed entity we can grasp; the rainbow is empty of inherent existence, yet it still appears.

Our sense of self is like this. Our sense of self appears to be real and continuous, yet it depends entirely on mental and physical conditions—thoughts, memories, sensations, and perceptions—constantly arising and dissolving. There is no singular, unchanging solid self at the center of our experience, only a fluid, shifting process that we habitually mistake for something fixed.

Yet just as we do not need to eliminate a rainbow to recognize its insubstantiality, we do not need to get rid of the self to recognize it as empty, but we only need to see through the illusion of its solidity. When we investigate it, the subjective aspect of experience has no qualities or characteristics whatsoever. The subjective aspect of experience is empty of all characteristics yet it is not nothing, because it is aware. There is a knowing presence that remains. With this insight, we recognize what the tradition calls *Awareness-Emptiness.*

## 2. The Emptiness of Phenomena – Everything is Empty

In the next stage of Insight Meditation, we extend our realization beyond the self to perceive that all phenomena are likewise empty of inherent existence. Rather than simply exploring the subjective aspect of experience, we explore the objective aspect of experience. This practice directly engages with the events that arise as perceptual phenomena and mental content. When these events are viewed through the lens of emptiness we dissolve the illusion of a fixed, static reality "out there."

Insight into the nature of phenomena also reveals the interdependent, fluid nature of all experience. Nāgārjuna, the great Madhyamaka philosopher, taught this by describing the fact that everything we experience arises in dependence on other conditions. This means there is no phenomenon that exists independently or in isolation. This insight dismantles our habitual way of seeing. The result of this practice shows:

- **Objects appear solid**, but they are composed of ever-changing particles, dependent on causes and conditions. What we call "a thing" is merely a conceptual label imposed on a shifting pattern of elements.

- **Thoughts seem real**, yet they are momentary flashes of mental activity, vanishing the instant they arise. No thought has intrinsic substance for it is simply the movement of awareness itself.

- **Time and space feel fixed**, yet they are mental constructs, frameworks imposed by the mind to organize experience. Past, present, and future do not exist as separate realities, but only as dependent designations.

Through Insight Meditation, we train the mind to see through these habitual perceptions, realizing that all appearances arise dependently, without intrinsic essence. In other words, all phenomena are empty. With this insight, we recognize what the tradition calls *Appearance-Emptiness.*

Even emptiness itself is empty; it is not an object, not a thing to grasp, but a way of seeing that dismantles all conceptual fixation. This insight does not lead to nihilism. It opens our heart to deeper compassion and interconnectedness, it dissolves any remaining clinging and reactivity, and it allows us to engage life with greater openness, fluidity, and wisdom.

## Interdependence and Compassion

This understanding of emptiness naturally gives rise to a profound realization of interdependence. When we see that nothing exists on its own—not the self, not objects, not even time or space—we begin to feel into the deep relationality of all things. Everything we experience arises through a web of conditions: physical, mental, emotional, cultural, and environmental. Everything is in relationship with everything else. This is not just a philosophical idea; it becomes a lived experience. The boundaries between self and other, inner and outer, begin to dissolve. We see that our well-being is inseparable from the well-being of others.

From this view, compassion becomes the most natural response. When there is no solid, isolated self, there is also no isolated suffering and no isolated joy. What affects one, affects the whole. The more clearly we see the emptiness of phenomena, the more we come to appreciate the intimate connectedness of all life. This interdependence becomes the source of great beauty and purpose. It invites us to care, to serve, and to live in a way that benefits the whole.

Thus, emptiness is not a cold or abstract negation. It is a doorway into love. It liberates us from grasping, and at the same time, it softens the heart. It frees us from the illusion of separation and opens us to the tender truth that we belong to each other. In this way, wisdom and compassion together form the natural expression of a mind that sees clearly and a heart that is open.

## The Third Turning: Buddha-Nature: Our True Nature (Tathagatagarbha)

If the First Turning of the Wheel of Dharma reveals the fundamental problem of impermanence, suffering, and non-self, and the Second Turning helps us see through confusion by realizing emptiness and interdependence, then the Third Turning reveals what remains when all obscurations fall away: our innate Buddha-Nature.

## Buddha-Nature – The Ever-Present Sky of Awareness

Buddha-Nature (*Tathāgatagarbha*) is the recognition that our true nature is always present and already awakened. The mind is like the sunlit sky: vast, boundless, and luminous. Although thoughts and emotions are constantly appearing and dissolving, they are like clouds, never altering the sky itself. No matter how dense the clouds may seem, the clarity of the sky remains untouched beneath them.

This teaching does not contradict emptiness, it completes it. Emptiness is not a mere negation or void; it is the space in which luminous, knowing awareness naturally shines. Buddha-Nature means that enlightenment is not something we create. We simply recognize it. Just as the sun does not need to be manufactured but only revealed when clouds part, Awakening is not an achievement but the unveiling of what has always been present when all the layers of obscuration are seen through.

## Nondual Realization

At the higher levels of insight, the distinction between awareness and appearances dissolves. What was once perceived as subject and object, observer and observed, is now recognized as an inseparable unity. *Awareness-emptiness and appearance-emptiness are not two separate aspects of experience, but two expressions of the very same awareness.* Both awareness-emptiness and appearance-emptiness are the same "taste" of emptiness. When this insight fully dawns, all perceived boundaries vanish, revealing the nondual nature of awareness-itself.

At this stage of insight, awareness is not something separate from appearances, nor are appearances independent from awareness. Rather than clinging to emptiness as mere negation or to appearances as something real, we abide in the natural state of nondual awareness, where emptiness and form are seamlessly one. Every experience is now recognized as the dynamic display of the mind's luminous clarity, unfolding without separation or obstruction. Awareness itself is inseparable from what appears, just as waves are never separate from the ocean or as the breeze is never separate from the sky. In this realization, there is nothing to hold onto and nothing to reject but there is only the effortless, self-arising dance of reality as it is.

The stages of nondual realization represent the highest integration of wisdom. In the next chapter, we'll unpack the levels of awareness and the gradations of nonduality according to Mahamudra. Ultimately, the practice of insight leads to the highest level of non-dual awareness: Awakened Awareness.

## Recognizing Our True Nature: Awakened Awareness

Our essential awareness is already awake, but it is temporarily obscured by confusion, grasping, and habitual misperception. The ultimate goal of Insight Meditation is to remove the obscurations that prevent us from recognizing our true nature. When we stop identifying with even the subtlest layers of confusion, we realize the natural clarity and wisdom that has been here all along.

The highest teachings of Mahamudra and Dzogchen emphasize "resting" directly in Awakened Awareness because what we seek is not separate from us. There is no need to fabricate or attain anything new; instead, we cultivate recognition of what is already unborn, unceasing, and fully present in each moment.

## The Healthy Functions of a Sense of Self

It's important to remember that even at the profound levels of nondual realization described above, errors in the practice can still occur. One of the errors that sometimes happens at this level of Insight Meditation is a failure to fully integrate the relative self.

As mentioned, in Insight Meditation we do not need to get rid of or erase the self just as we do not need to erase rainbows from the sky. In fact, a healthy nondual realization allows space for the self that still *seems to exist*. The problem that obscures Awakened Awareness is not the appearance of self, the obscuring problem is a failure to recognize that even the self is the display of empty awareness.

Why is the relative self important?

On the relative level, the self is vital.

## A Healthy Sense of Self Plays an Important Role

A healthy relative self serves several essential functions. First, it provides an organizing principle for experience. The self acts as a central reference point, allowing us to track our own growth and plan for the future. Without this structure, thoughts and emotions would be fragmented, making it difficult to function in daily life.

Second, it offers consistency across states and time. A well-integrated self provides stability, enabling us to maintain a coherent identity even as circumstances change. This consistency fosters resilience, helping us stay grounded during difficulties.

Third, a healthy self is a structure that can grow, adapt, and mature. It is not a rigid entity but an evolving process of development. As it matures, it allows us to move beyond ego-centered concerns toward a broader, more compassionate way of being.

Fourth, it serves as a vehicle for unique skills, gifts, and expression. Each person has distinctive strengths and insights that can benefit others. The goal is not to erase individuality but to align it with wisdom, so our personal gifts contribute to the greater good.

Finally, the self functions as a bridge between relative and ultimate reality. It acts as an interface between absolute reality—emptiness and pure awareness—and relative experience. This allows us to engage in relationships, ethics, and responsibilities without becoming lost in self-clinging.

## The Dangers of Not Integrating the Self: Dissociation, Depersonalization, and Derealization

While Insight Meditation is often associated with greater well-being and self-awareness, when pursued without healthy psychological integration, it can lead to serious dissociative states. These states of dissociation, depersonalization, and derealization often arise when deep emotional wounds, trauma, or unconscious material are bypassed rather than integrated.

## Dissociation: Splitting from Experience

Dissociation is a disconnection from thoughts, emotions, body sensations, or even a sense of self. It can manifest as feeling emotionally numb, spaced out, or disconnected from reality. Rather than working through pain, dissociation creates a psychic split where difficult emotions or memories are pushed out of awareness.

Some meditation practitioners, especially those engaged in high-intensity retreats or prolonged concentration practices, may unknowingly reinforce dissociative tendencies rather than resolving them. When meditation becomes a tool to escape rather than integrate, practitioners may feel increasingly detached from their emotions, relationships, or the world itself.

## Depersonalization: Losing the Sense of "Me"

Depersonalization is the experience of feeling unreal or estranged from one's own body and identity. People in this state often describe feeling like they are watching themselves from the outside, as if life is happening to someone else. This can be triggered by trauma but can also emerge from spiritual practices that deconstruct the sense of self without simultaneously cultivating embodiment and integration.

In some non-dual or emptiness-based teachings, there is a risk of misunderstanding selflessness as a negation of all personal identity rather than an integration of self and emptiness. Without grounding in healthy selfhood, practitioners may mistake depersonalization for spiritual progress, failing to recognize the underlying fragmentation.

## Derealization: The World Feels Unreal

Derealization is the sense that the external world is dreamlike, distant, or artificial. Colors may seem faded, time may feel distorted, and interactions may feel devoid of emotional significance. This often arises when a person is overwhelmed by stress or trauma and unconsciously disengages from reality as a protective mechanism.

In meditation, particularly when practices emphasize deconstructing ordinary perception without stabilizing practices like *metta* (loving-kindness) or grounding techniques, derealization can emerge as an unintended side effect. Rather than Awakening to the vibrancy of reality, a practitioner may feel more and more detached from it.

## How to Mitigate Against Adverse Effects of Meditation

The Cheetah House project, founded by Dr. Willoughby Britton, has been at the forefront of studying the adverse effects of Insight Meditation. Through her research, Britton has documented numerous cases of meditators who developed dissociation, depersonalization, or extreme anxiety due to intensive meditation practice without proper support. Her work emphasizes the importance of:

- **Balancing insight practices with grounding techniques** to avoid excessive deconstruction of the self.

- **Recognizing that meditation is not inherently right for everyone**, especially those with trauma histories or psychological vulnerabilities.

- **Providing psychological support for meditators** who experience unintended negative effects.

Her findings challenge the romanticized idea that meditation is always beneficial, showing instead that when practiced improperly or without adequate preparation, it can exacerbate psychological instability instead of resolving it.

## Integrating the Self

A truly holistic path of insight involves deep integration. Healthy Insight Meditation does not suppress or bypass the personal self but rather refines, heals, and integrates it into a larger, more expansive awareness.

This may mean that the path intentionally includes practicing embodiment through movement, breathwork, or body-awareness practices alongside meditation. These embodied approaches help ground insight in lived experience, making the path more sustainable and whole.

It likely also means that healthy approaches to Insight Meditation include trauma-sensitive methods that prioritize psychological safety and respect the unique needs of each practitioner. Rather than dismissing the self, this approach recognizes the importance of cultivating a healthy sense of self as a stable and resilient foundation. When integrated in this way, the personal self becomes a vessel for deeper Awakening, not something to eliminate, but something to illuminate.

If you notice dissociation or any of the other adverse effects listed above, pause the Insight Meditation practice and seek support. There may be certain psychological factors to put in place through love, self-compassion, and tenderness, before you go back to the practice.

As the American Buddhist and psychotherapist, Jack Engler, put it: "You have to be somebody before you are nobody."

### Closing Reflection: Seeing Through and Seeing Beyond

So I invite you to reflect on a few questions related to Insight Meditation:

- What happens when you see the self as a process rather than a thing?

- How would your life change if you trusted that your Buddha-Nature was already present?

- What would it be like to live in nondual awareness all of the time?

### Looking Ahead

In the next chapter, we will explore Mahamudra and Dzogchen, the pinnacle of Tibetan teachings.

For now, simply remember:

*Insight is not about changing reality, but about seeing through the veils obscuring your true nature.*

## Chapter 14

# MAHAMUDRA AND DZOGCHEN

### The Path to Full Enlightenment

At the culmination of the path, there are two profound approaches to bring the meditator to full realization: Mahamudra and Dzogchen.

Mahamudra and Dzogchen represent the pinnacle teachings in different schools within the Tibetan tradition. Each system reveals the nature of mind and nurtures that realization to full enlightenment.

Both Mahamudra and Dzogchen provide a path to full enlightenment:

- **Mahamudra (The Great Seal)** emphasizes the recognition that all experiences, all perceptions, and even the mind itself bear the great seal of emptiness and awareness.

- **Dzogchen (The Great Perfection)** emphasizes that the nature of mind has never been defiled for it is primordially pure, already perfect, and already free.

In his classic 17th century text, *The Union of Mahamudra and Dzogchen*, Karma Chagme describes Mahamudra and Dzogchen as the most profound level of teachings. He writes:

*"There are many philosophical viewpoints and many dif-*
*ferent systems of teachings, but actually there is nothing which*
*is not included within Mahamudra and Dzogchen. Just as*
*all things are contained within space, likewise, all the other*
*viewpoints and systems are included within these two. Since*
*these two are essentially the same, condensing everything into*
*a single practice is most profound."*

The difference between Mahamudra and Dzogchen is in method not ground or result. The ground of
Mahamudra and Dzogchen is the same reality: primordially pure, clear and empty awareness. The path may
differ in method and emphasis. The fruition is identical: the full recognition of Enlightened Awareness.

Below, we examine both Mahamudra and Dzogchen in a bit more detail. We start with Mahamudra.

## Three Approaches to Mahamudra:
## Sutra, Tantra, and Essence

Mahamudra is practiced through three distinct approaches, each suited to different temperaments and levels of readiness: Sutra Mahamudra (Gradual Path), Tantra Mahamudra (Empowerment and Deity Yoga), and
Essence Mahamudra (Direct Introduction). While each
method differs in its approach, all ultimately lead to the
same realization of the mind's luminous, empty nature.

### Sutra Mahamudra: The Gradual Approach

Sutra Mahamudra is the closest to what we've described so far with our chapters on concentration meditation and insight meditation. Sutra Mahamudra follows
a structured method, emphasizing a step-by-step path of
purification and meditative development. The traditional approach to Sutra Mahamudra is rooted in:

- *Shamatha* (**calm abiding**) to cultivate
  sustained attention and mental tranquility.

- *Vipaśyanā* (**insight meditation**) using conceptual analysis and direct meditative investigation to recognize one's true nature.

Through systematic practice, the meditator gradually refines perception and insight, leading to direct recognition of Awakened Awareness.

## Tantra Mahamudra: The Empowered Path

Tantra Mahamudra operates within the Vajrayana framework, utilizing empowerments, deity yoga, and subtle energy practices to rapidly accelerate realization. This path includes:

- **Receiving empowerment** (*abhisheka*) to ripen the mind for direct experience.

- **Visualization and mantra recitation** to dissolve habitual conceptual fixation.

- **Inner yogas** (such as Tummo or the Six Yogas of Naropa) to dissolve ordinary perception and reveal the mind's innate radiance.

Through these methods, Tantra Mahamudra transforms perception from the inside out, allowing realization to unfold more swiftly than the gradual path.

## Essence Mahamudra: The Direct Introduction

Essence Mahamudra bypasses gradual development and introduces the practitioner directly to the nature of mind through the transmission of an authentic master. Essence Mahamudra can be taught as a stand alone approach. Or it can be combined with Sutra or Tantra Mahamudra. Essence Mahamudra is characterized by:

- **Direct pointing-out instructions**, where the teacher reveals the nature of awareness.

- **Resting in recognition**, without the need for

extensive analysis or conceptual meditation.

- **Stabilizing realization through continuous familiarization**, rather than structured methods.

The essence approach is the most immediate and direct, yet it requires the right conditions: a qualified master, a receptive student, and strong karmic readiness.

## Different Paths, Same Realization

All three approaches—Sutra, Tantra, and Essence Mahamudra—lead to the same realization of Awakened Awareness: the union of emptiness and awareness. The gradual Sutra path provides a structured foundation, the Tantric path accelerates the process through skillful means, and the Essence path reveals realization directly. Each practitioner must find the approach that best suits their disposition, level of trust, and karmic ripening.

## Levels of Awareness in Mahamudra

Awareness is so intimately woven into our experience that we rarely question its nature. In the gradual path of Mahamudra in particular, the practices help us investigate the layers of the mind with precision and clarity. As investigation unfolds, the practice reveals progressively deeper levels of awareness. These levels of awareness have always been present but often go unnoticed or unrecognized.

Depending on the divisions made, there are at least five levels of awareness revealed through gradual Mahamudra Practice. I'll first name the levels of awareness and then we will explore how each level relates to a specific stage of practice.

## <u>Level 0</u>: Ordinary Deluded Mind

The average person spends most of their waking

hours in the default mode, moving through life on auto-pilot without conscious awareness. We can call this default mode the Ordinary Deluded Mind and label it as Level 0. It is scattered and easily distracted, drifting aimlessly between thoughts, emotions, and external stimuli without discernment. This level of awareness is reactive, self-referential, and driven by habitual patterns rather than intentional clarity.

## Level 1: Awareness

At this stage, awareness begins to recognize that it is separate from thought. Through concentration practice, moments arise where thought subsides, yet an alert, knowing presence remains. Instead of being lost in the stream of thinking, awareness can simply rest, clear and undistracted. The level of mind feels more stable, present, and at ease, no longer compulsively chasing thoughts but observing them with a sense of alert presence. This shift marks a fundamental realization: awareness is not the same as thought but it is now known directly as something deeper, always present beneath mental activity. My teacher, Dan Brown, referred to this stage of practice as shifting from "thought-mode" to "awareness-mode."

## Level 2: Spacious Awareness

As practice deepens, awareness further disentangles itself, not only from thought but also from the sense of a fixed, personal self. Rather than experiencing awareness as something located inside the head or behind the eyes, it begins to feel much more spacious. Thoughts, emotions, sensations, visual forms, and auditory sounds arise and dissolve like clouds in an open sky, but awareness itself remains unchanged. A deep ease emerges as the burden of self-concern and reactivity starts to fade, revealing a more expansive and inclusive way of being.

## Level 3: Changeless-Boundless Awareness

With continued practice, the illusion of awareness being tied to time and space begins to dissolve. There is a growing recognition that awareness is not something that comes and goes but it has always been here, untouched by the movement of experience. Even as thoughts, emotions, and perceptions arise and pass away, awareness itself remains constant, boundless, and free. This level of awareness brings a profound sense of stillness and stability, as one sees that awareness is not something personal or fleeting, but an ever-present, unchanging ground. This level of awareness feels truly wide open and vast.

## Level 4: Nondual Awareness

At this stage, the division between observer and observed dissolves. Awareness is no longer experienced as something separate from what arises within it since everything that arises is recognized as awareness. Sensory experiences, thoughts, and emotions are no longer seen as occurring to a subject but are recognized as spontaneous expressions of the same awareness doing the observing. When the boundary between subject and object disappears entirely, an all-pervasive presence is revealed. Reality appears vivid and immediate, yet without any separation, bringing a profound sense of intimacy with all that is.

## Level 5: Awakened Awareness (*Rigpa*)

In the culminating level of awareness, all effort, grasping, and conceptualization fall away. Awareness is no longer sourced in a center or location. There is no particular place awareness is coming from. Awareness is everywhere and nowhere in particular. Awareness is lucid, vast, all pervasive, and centerless. There is no meditator and nothing to meditate on, yet awareness remains effortlessly awake and boundless. Experience flows freely without resistance, and there is a deep sense of ease, as all notions of limitation, selfhood, or striving have been fully seen through. This is not a state to attain but the recognition of what has always been present, beyond all obscuration.

So, to review, here are the basic levels of awareness summarized:

**Level 0**: **Ordinary Deluded Mind** (default mode)

**Level 1**: **Awareness**

**Level 2**: **Spacious Awareness**

**Level 3**: **Changeless-Boundless Awareness**

**Level 4**: **Non-dual Awareness**

**Level 5**: **Awakened Awareness**

Awakened Awareness (Level 5) is what we've been referring to throughout this book as your true nature. Awakened Awareness is the ground of being itself. Although the phrase "waking up" refers to the whole sequence as one moves from Level 0 to Level 5, the term "Awakening" in particular refers to recognizing Awakened Awareness. It is Awakened Awareness that we stabilize and nurture to full Buddhahood.

## States vs. Vantage Points

One important distinction to mention here is the difference between a shift in state and a shift in vantage point. Each time you access a new level of awareness, you shift your basis of operation. Your basic experience of where awareness is coming from changes. This is called a shift in vantage point. I've written about this extensively elsewhere and suggest the reader go to my other books for details. For now, I'll discuss the distinction only briefly.

**Shifts in State** relate to changes in the field of experience.

**Shifts in Vantage Points** refer to a change in where awareness is coming from.

Realization is not about having a new state experience. All states come and go. Awakening doesn't add something new to experience. Awakening is about shifting through the levels of awareness to recognize what is most fundamental, Awakened Awareness. Whether it occurs suddenly or gradually, Awakening involves seeing through layers of confusion to reveal a deeper level of awareness that's already here. From this perspective, shifting to Awakened Awareness, or more accurately recognizing Awakened Awareness is the deepest of all vantage points. It is that which remains when all the layers of obscuration are removed.

The essential point is this: States constantly change. Vantage Points can be stabilized.

One of the easiest ways to make the distinction between a state and a vantage point in your own direct experience is to focus on certain questions and avoiding others. Rather than looking for some change in the experience and asking, "What has changed in the field of experience", an even better question to ask yourself is "what level of awareness am I coming from?."

This means it is not enough to simply be mindful of the content of our experience. Instead, we have to ask ourselves, "What is my vantage point?." Or as Dan Brown used to often ask us, "What is your basis of operation?"

You can be mindful as a tiny pinhole (Level 1: Awareness) or you can be mindful as the vast ocean (Level 3: Changeless-Boundless Awareness). The difference in these two perspectives is not what arises in experience. The content might be identical. The difference is what level of awareness are you being mindful from? The level of awareness you are coming from makes all the difference in the world.

## The Four Yogas of Mahamudra

Gampopa, the great Mahamudra master, described the progressive unfolding of realization through The Four Yogas of Mahamudra. Each yoga clarifies a confusion/obscuration and shifts the student's vantage point through the levels of awareness. In the following outline, I'll show how each of these Four Yogas in the gradual approach to Mahamudra, align with the levels of awareness we've just covered.

## The Yoga of One-Pointedness: Concentration Meditation

Before practice, the mind is scattered, reactive, and easily distracted. This is the ordinary deluded mind operating in its default mode, known as Level 0. Concentration practice begins with stabilizing the mind by learning to rest one-pointedly on the meditation object. As distraction subsides, the practitioner develops an unwavering presence that is no longer susceptible to external or internal disturbances. Through this practice, the meditator shifts from being caught in discursive thought to operating from stable awareness. This marks the transition to Awareness, or Level 1.

## The Yoga of Non-Elaboration: Basic Emptiness Meditation

In this yoga, the meditator uses their new capacity for sustained focus to investigate the nature of self, perception, and mental content. At this stage the practitioner uses the lens of emptiness to see through all levels of phenomena until none of the events in each category can obscure the nature of awareness. As conceptual labels fall away, the mind stops categorizing experiences as good or bad, pleasant or unpleasant. The vantage point revealed here transcends the habitual confusion of reifying a separate self "in here" and an external world of events "out there." This leads to an experience of awareness that is increasingly open and spacious, known as Spacious Awareness, or Level 2.

At the later stages of this yoga, perception moves beyond the limitations of time and space, revealing a level of awareness without edges or boundaries, and that doesn't come and go in time. This is Changeless-Boundless Awareness, or Level 3. At this stage, all phenomena appear within the vast field of ever-present awareness, and the meditator comes to a direct recognition that they are this spacious, unconditioned presence.

## The Yoga of One Taste: Establishing Nonduality

In this yoga, any remaining separation between subject and object dissolves. All experiences, whether sights, sounds, smells, tastes, sensations, thoughts, and emotions, are recognized as the "same taste" of emptiness or the "one taste" of awareness. This vantage point sees beyond the confusion of dualistic awareness, revealing a more unified way of perceiving reality.

In the middle stages of the Yoga of One Taste, awareness becomes all-pervasive. Awareness seamlessly pervades everything. At this stage, because you are no longer caught in the limitations of duality, you are coming from or being this all-pervasive awareness.

By the later stages of this yoga, maintaining this nondual awareness is effortless since it is simply the natural way of being. The Level of Awareness revealed in the Yoga of One Taste is Nondual Awareness (Level 4).

## The Yoga of Non-Meditation: Refining in Effortlessness and Recognizing Awakened Awareness

In this final yoga, all residual effort dissolves. There is no "meditator" and nothing to "meditate on", yet what remains is a crystal-clear, lucid field of awareness. No longer seeking or grasping, awareness naturally abides in its own nature.

In the early stages of the Yoga of Non-Meditation, you are coming from a level of awareness that is completely at rest, wide open, and naturally free. At the late stages of Non-Meditation, all sense of localization drops away. Awareness is no longer bound to any fixed point of reference.

Awakened Awareness does not have a center or source, yet it is a lucid knowing that is everywhere all at once. The Level of Awareness revealed in the Yoga of Non-Meditation is Awakened Awareness (Level 5).

This progression in Mahamudra moves from effort to effortlessness, from stabilizing attention, to dissolving reification of self and phenomena, to recognizing the same taste of all events, and finally to simply resting in the natural state of mind and recognizing our true nature as Awakened Awareness. It's a profound path. The Four Yogas show you the path all the way home.

## Dzogchen and the Three Statements of Garab Dorje

Dzogchen, or the Great Perfection, is structured differently than Mahamudra, yet both traditions ultimately lead to the same realization: the direct recognition of an awakened mind.

The heart of Dzogchen is based on direct transmission. A Dzogchen master guides the student by directly introducing them to Awakened Awareness. In this way, the directness of Dzogchen is most similar to Essence Mahamudra.

One of the central and most popular teachings in Dzogchen is the Three Statements of Garab Dorje, the first human teacher of the tradition. These three pith instructions encapsulate the entire Dzogchen path:

1. **Direct Introduction to the Nature of Mind** (Recognize Awakened Awareness)

2. **Decide on One Thing** (Stabilize Awakened Awareness in all times and all situations)

3. **Continue in Confidence in Liberation** (Bringing the Path to Full Buddhahood and Completion)

The first step is the **Direct Introduction to the Nature of Mind**. In this first stage the teacher directly introduces the student to their own Awakened Awareness, or rigpa. In this moment, the student recognizes their natural state just as it is, free from conceptual elaboration. This is the ground aspect of Awakening.

The second step is to **Decide on One Thing**. At this stage the practitioner learns to stabilize Awakened Awareness in all times and situations. Once awareness is recognized, a firm decision is made that this awareness appears as everything. This realization must pervade every moment of experience until Awakening is fully stabilized.

The final step is to **Continue in Confidence in Liberation**. This stage brings the path to full Buddhahood and completion. Here, the practitioner trusts fully in what has already been revealed. There is nothing to alter or change; everything is left exactly as it is, liberating itself by itself. As karmic conditioning is exhausted, all positive aspects of the mind naturally blossom, revealing the fullness of an enlightened mind.

These three statements famously sum up the entire path of Dzogchen. Unlike approaches that refine understanding over time, Dzogchen is radically direct: one either recognizes the awakened mind or does not. In any moment, *including right now*, you are either recognizing *rigpa* (Awakened Awareness) or are in *ma-rigpa* (non-awareness). The task is not to accumulate knowledge but to deepen certainty and confidence, allowing naturalness of Awakened Awareness to blossom until full enlightenment is complete.

## The Waxing Moon of Enlightenment

The word Awakening, as I use it, refers to the direct experience of our true nature, Awakened Awareness. Even if fleeting, a direct experience of Awakened Awareness is incredibly liberating. Enlightenment, on the other hand, is reserved for when we learn to stabilize the recognition of Awakened Awareness in all times and situations. This includes nurturing the Awakening and bringing it to its full fruition. For most of us, Enlightenment unfolds much like the phases of the moon, revealing itself gradually. In the beginning, we get a little taste of Awakening. This is like catching a glimpse of the crescent moon in the sky. This glimpse is real and beautiful for we are actually seeing the moon. But even though the glimpse is authentic and precious, the crescent moon is not yet full. Much of the moon remains shrouded in shadow.

In the same way, an early taste of Awakening, whether it comes through meditation, deep contemplation, or through the transmission of a teacher, does not mean full enlightenment has dawned. Even as clarity breaks through, there are still unseen patterns, unconscious wounds, and subtle attachments that remain in darkness. There is still healing to be done, still integration required to bring the wisdom of insight fully into our being. This means that even after a glimpse of Awakening, the view must then be stabilized *in all times and in all situations and brought to its fullest fruition.*

As the moon waxes and as the stabilization of Awakening deepens, more of the moon's light becomes visible, and the beauty of its form becomes clearer. Likewise, with each step of ever deepening Awakening, our ability to hold the world in compassion expands and our perception clarifies.

Finally, the full moon shines with no part of the moon remaining in shadow. This is the full moon of enlightenment, when every karmic trace and obscuration has dissolved. Love is naturally and spontaneously boundless, Enlightened Awareness is naturally and spontaneously effortless, and all appearances are naturally and spontaneously recognized as the radiant expression of an enlightened mind.

As my teacher Dan Brown would often say at this stage of realization, the direct experience is that "Primordial Wisdom expresses itself to itself for the sake of its own realization."

## The Meaning of Full Enlightenment (Sangye)

The ultimate purpose of Mahamudra and Dzogchen is the complete realization of Full Enlightenment. This is called *Sangye* or full Buddhahood, the total flowering of wisdom and compassion.

The Tibetan word *Sangye* expresses both the purification of all obscurations and the full development of wisdom and compassion.

- **"San"** means purified of all karmic obscurations, grasping, and distortions..

- **"Gye"** means the blossoming of wisdom and compassion have reached their full expression.

This is not the annihilation of experience, nor is

it an escape from the world. It is the complete clarifying of experience, where all that was once perceived through the filter of ignorance and karmic obscuration is now seen as it truly is, the luminous display of an enlightened mind.

With full enlightenment, there is no longer a fragmented or dualistic perception of reality filtered through a karmic lens. What was once seen as self and other, inside and outside, *samsara* and *nirvana*, is now known to be the indivisible play of Enlightened Awareness itself.

## Closing Reflection: Recognizing the Full Moon of Enlightened Awareness

Instead of treating these teachings as concepts to analyze, take a moment to begin to directly experience what they are pointing to:

- Where is your awareness coming from right now? Is it something you can grasp? Can you find any edges or boundaries to awareness?

- Is there truly a boundary between your "self" and world, or are all experiences simply appearing in an open field of awareness itself?

- What happens if you stop searching, stop analyzing, and simply allow everything to be exactly as it is?

The full moon of enlightenment is not something you need to chase after, nor is it something far away. Just as the full moon is always present, even when hidden by clouds, the nature of your mind is already awake, already luminous. It only needs to be recognized.

You are not moving toward Awakening, you are simply removing the clouds that obscure it. Mahamudra and Dzogchen are the pinnacle approaches to bring the path to its completion.

In the next chapter, we will explore how a buddha integrates enlightenment into daily life.

For now, simply remember:

*Mahamudra and Dzogchen reveal what was never lost—your own enlightened mind.*

Chapter 15

# THE WISDOM ENERGIES AND BUDDHA BODIES

## The Unending Activity of Enlightenment

In the previous chapter, we explored Mahamudra and Dzogchen, the culmination of the path, where full enlightenment is realized. But enlightenment doesn't mean that everything disappears. Enlightenment is the end of all seeking but it is the beginning of an unceasing refinement of compassionate activity. *Perfect emptiness is perfect intimacy with reality.*

At this stage, from the perspective of wisdom there is no longer a fixed self that acts, nor separate beings to help. Yet, from the perspective of compassion, activity continues effortlessly and inexhaustibly because there are still beings who appear and believe they are confused. So although an enlightened mind sees things the way that they *are*, an enlightened heart understands how things *appear.* And in this way, the two wings of enlightenment, wisdom and compassion, allow a Buddha to soar.

The infinite expression of enlightened activity can be further understood through two aspects: The Five Wisdom Energies and The Buddha Bodies.

These two aspects will serve as the core focus of this chapter. Let's start with the basics:

- **The Five Wisdom Energies** reveal how emotions and experiences are transformed into enlightened expressions.

- **The Buddha Bodies** (*Trikaya*) describe how enlightened presence manifests in different dimensions of reality all at once to benefit beings.

The teachings on the Wisdom Energies and Buddha Bodies help us understand that enlightenment is not merely an internal realization but a living force actively expressed in the world. A Buddha does not manifest as a static being but as an ever-present, responsive field of wisdom, dynamically engaged with all circumstances. The work of benefiting beings is inexhaustible because it is the natural radiance of enlightenment itself, effortlessly arising from the ground of awakened awareness.

In this way, enlightenment is not an escape but allows a profound and skillful engagement with all of reality.

## The Five Wisdom Energies—Transforming the Mind into Enlightened Expression

The Five Wisdom Energies describe the fundamental patterns of experience and how they are transformed into the enlightened qualities of the Buddhas. The five wisdoms are: (1) Mirror-like, (2) Equanimity/Sameness, (3) Discriminating, (4) All-Accomplishing, and (5) Dharmadhatu.

### From Delusion to Wisdom

The Five Wisdom Energies exist in both deluded and enlightened states, shaping our experience of reality.

In ignorance, these energies appear as distorted emotions and self-clinging, manifesting as anger, pride, attachment, competitiveness, or confusion. These very same energies, when skillfully engaged on the tantric path, become the raw material for transformation. Rather than suppressing or rejecting them, the practitioner intentionally refines and transmutes these emotions into their higher expressions, revealing their deeper wisdom. In the full fruition of enlightenment, these energies manifest as the five spontaneously present fundamental wisdoms of a Buddha or radiant expressions of clarity, equanimity, deep understanding, skillful action, and vast openness.

Each wisdom energy is intrinsically connected to a natural element, reflecting its samsaric distortion as well as its awakened potential. Water, earth, fire, wind, and space each serve as metaphors for the dynamic unfolding of these energies, showing how rigidity can become clarity, greed can become generosity, attachment can become deep love, striving can become effortless action, and confusion can become vast, luminous awareness. When fully realized, these energies no longer bind us; instead, they unfold into their pure expressions, the enlightened wisdom of a buddha.

Let's go through each of the Wisdom Energies one by one.

## Mirror-like Wisdom Energy – Clarity and Precision (Water Element)

Mirror-like Wisdom energy, like the water element, is sharp, reflective, and penetrating, cutting through illusion with intellect and clarity. In its distorted form, this energy can freeze into coldness, anger, and rigid judgment, becoming an unyielding force that dismisses warmth and compassion. Like ice, it becomes harsh and unrelenting, isolating itself in an attempt to maintain control. However, when transformed, this energy reveals a clarity as pure and reflective as still water, perfectly mirroring reality without distortion or bias. Just as a calm lake reflects the sky, this wisdom allows one to see things exactly as they are, without personal projections or emotional turbulence. It brings precision without cruelty, truth without rigidity, and discernment that sees through illusion with compassionate clarity. A Buddha expressing this energy is in perfect harmony with the fluid, unobstructed nature of water, embodying its depth, transparency, and boundless capacity to reflect reality.

## Equanimity Wisdom – Richness and Stability (Earth Element)

Equanimity Wisdom energy, like the earth element, embodies stability, nourishment, and abundance. It provides a foundation for growth, a sense of solidity amidst change. It is sometimes called the Wisdom of Sameness. In its distorted form, it can harden into pride, overindulgence, and hoarding, clinging to wealth, knowledge, or status out of a fear of loss. This fixation creates a sense of entitlement, as if one must fortify oneself against the impermanence of life. However, when transformed, this energy expresses the deep, unshakable stability of the earth, which holds and includes the preciousness of all beings without bias. Rather than grasping at accumulation, it radiates generosity and trust, recognizing that true wealth lies in the ability to nourish and uplift others. This wisdom brings a deep groundedness, confidence, and natural inclusion, offering its gifts as effortlessly as the earth provides sustenance. A Buddha expressing this energy is in perfect harmony with the solid, abundant nature of earth, embodying its capacity to support, nurture, and sustain all beings.

## Discriminating Wisdom – Passion and Magnetism (Fire Element)

Discriminating Wisdom energy, like the fire element,

is radiant, passionate, and magnetic, drawing beings together through warmth and connection. In its distorted form, it flares into attachment, clinging, and addiction, grasping at pleasure, relationships, or experiences in a desperate attempt to feel whole. Just as uncontrolled fire can consume everything in its path, unbalanced Discriminating Wisdom energy burns with longing, obsession, and manipulation, seeking fulfillment through external validation. When transformed, this wisdom is bright, illuminating a flame of deep understanding, unconditional love, and perfect intimacy with all form. Just as fire reveals and clarifies, this wisdom sees the unique essence of each person and situation, fostering genuine connection without possessiveness. In its awakened form, Discriminating Wisdom energy inspires, magnetizes, and radiates warmth, offering a presence that ignites love, intimacy, and appreciation in all beings. A Buddha expressing this energy is in perfect harmony with the illuminating and transformative power of fire, embodying its radiance, brilliance, and ability to burn away all separation.

## All-Accomplishing Wisdom – Action and Accomplishment (Wind Element)

All-Accomplishing wisdom energy, like the wind element, is dynamic, swift, and full of movement, driving action and transformation. In its distorted form, it manifests as competitiveness, envy, and manipulation, leading to restlessness and an obsessive need to control outcomes. Like a stormy wind that cannot be contained, it pushes forward relentlessly, always chasing achievement without ever arriving. This can make one forceful, impatient, and consumed by the need to win. However, when transformed, this energy reveals the spontaneous ability to act with precision, skill, and perfect timing, like the effortless flow of wind through space. Freed from grasping and comparison, movement arises fluidly, without struggle or ego-driven effort. This wisdom arises as compassionate leadership, intuitive action, and the ability to manifest change with ease. A Buddha expressing this energy is in perfect harmony with the unhindered, responsive nature of wind, moving with the natural currents of life without resistance or force.

## Dharmadhatu Wisdom– Spaciousness and Openness (Space Element)

Dharmadhatu Wisdom energy, like the space element, is vast, open, and all-encompassing, providing the groundless expanse within which all things arise and dissolve. In its distorted form, it manifests as ignorance, confusion, or dissociation, becoming lost in numbness or inertia. Like the emptiness of a sky covered in thick clouds, this unawakened state obscures the clarity and vastness beneath. However, when awakened, this energy expresses boundless, luminous awareness that holds everything with complete openness. This is the recognition that nothing needs to be rejected, nothing is separate from awareness itself. Like pure, infinite space, this wisdom brings profound peace, effortless presence, and a limitless capacity to embrace all experience. A buddha is in perfect harmony with the unbounded, all-pervading nature of space, resting in its vastness and infinite potential without fixation or struggle.

## The Five Wisdoms and Their Transformations

| Wisdom Energy | Element | Distorted (Samsaric) Expression | Transformed into |
|---|---|---|---|
| Mirror-Like Wisdom (Clarity, Precision) | Water | Coldness, Anger, Judgment | Perfect clarity, seeing reality as it is |
| Equanimity Wisdom (Preciousness, Sameness, Stability) | Earth | Pride, Overindulgence, Hoarding | Unshakable stability and inclusion |
| Discriminating Wisdom (Passion, Magnetism) | Fire | Attachment, Clinging, Addiction | Deep understanding, perfect intimacy with all form |
| All-Accomplishing Wisdom (Action, Accomplishment) | Wind | Competitiveness, Envy, Manipulation | Spontaneous, skillful action |
| Dharmadhatu Wisdom (Spaciousness, Openness) | Space | Ignorance, Confusion, Dissociation | Vast, all-encompassing openness |

## How the Five Wisdoms Manifest in an Enlightened Being

All Buddhas have access to the full spectrum of the Five Wisdom Energies. These energies are seamlessly integrated into a perfectly awakened expression as different facets of the same enlightened awareness.

A Buddha naturally expresses the clarity of Mirror-Like Wisdom, the stability of Equanimity, the warmth of Discriminating Awareness, the effortless activity of All-Accomplishing Wisdom, and the vast openness of Dharmadhatu Wisdom without any distortion or imbalance. Each wisdom manifests spontaneously as needed to serve the benefit of beings.

In this way, an enlightened mind sees clearly, loves fully, acts skillfully, and holds space for all beings.

## The Buddha Bodies (*Kayas*)

A Buddha's enlightened nature pervades all dimensions of experience, manifesting in different ways to guide beings toward Awakening. This is described through the teachings on Three Buddha Bodies (Tri-kaya). The Three Buddha Bodies reveal the inseparable unity of absolute reality, wisdom, and compassionate action. The bodies are: the *Dharmakaya*, the *Sambhogakaya*, and the *Nirmanakaya*.

Although these three facets are described using the term "bodies", it might be helpful to think of them as embodied layers or realms of existence.

The **Dharmakaya**, or *Body of Reality*, is the vast, infinite womb of enlightenment itself beyond form, beyond location, and beyond identity. The Dharmakaya is the ultimate ground of being, the space-like awareness that is perfectly empty yet the source of all experience. This is the awakened mind in its purest aspect, completely beyond birth, death, or change. Just as the sky remains untouched by clouds, the Dharmakaya is the stainless layer of existence, free from any obscuration. It remains ever-present as the true nature and home of all Buddhas.

The **Sambhogakaya**, or *Body of Bliss and Wisdom*, is the luminous radiance of enlightenment appearing as pure vision. This level of experience is revealed as the direct result of all karmic obscurations being purified. It includes both the energetic body in its purified form as well as the dimension of reality where wisdom manifests in the form of Buddhas, dakinis, and enlightened energy. This is the sacred dimension of reality. This is the realm of pure communication, symbolic meaning, and visionary experience where Enlightened Awareness expresses itself through wisdom forms that inspire and guide practitioners.

The **Nirmanakaya**, or *Emanation Body*, is the compassionate manifestation of enlightenment in and as the physical world. This is how Buddhas appear to others within samsara, taking forms that can directly engage with ordinary beings. The Nirmanakaya fully experiences the suffering of sentient beings, embodying their struggles while remaining anchored in the emptiness of the Dharmakaya and the sacredness of the Sambhogakaya. Enlightened beings emanate in countless ways, whether as great teachers or ordinary people, always adapting to the needs of those they serve.

Together, these three Buddha Bodies reveal that enlightenment is not a singular, static state but an all-pervading presence functioning on multiple levels of reality at once. A Buddha's experience is boundless and empty as Dharmakaya, luminous and sacred as Sambhogakaya, and compassionate and responsive as Nirmanakaya. These bodies are perfectly inseparable as one seamless whole. (This inseparability is sometimes called the Svabhāvikakāya or Essence body). The three Buddha Bodies show that enlightenment is fully present across all layers of existence for it flows through all dimensions of experience, manifesting in infinite ways to benefit all beings.

## Compassionate Expression Through Body, Speech, and Mind

With the Buddha Bodies stabilized and the Five Wisdom Energies spontaneously present, Enlightenment naturally expresses itself through the body, speech, and mind of a buddha.

These three dimensions of expression (body, speech, mind) allow the enlightened presence to engage dynamically with the world, benefiting beings in whatever way is needed.

## The Three Modes of a Buddha's Expression

The **Body** is the visible form of enlightenment. A Buddha's actions, movements, and gestures are not ordinary; they are direct transmissions of wisdom, effortlessly embodying compassion and clarity. Even the environment surrounding an enlightened being can become a field of transformation, radiating an energy that uplifts and awakens those who come into contact with it.

The **Speech** of a Buddha carries the liberating power of words, arising directly from awakened wisdom with the sole intention of benefiting all beings. A Buddha's teachings are never random; they are perfectly attuned to what each individual needs at any given moment. Sometimes speech is soft and gentle, offering encouragement and ease, while at other times it is sharp and direct, cutting through delusion. Even silence can be a profound teaching when it arises from deep realization, conveying truth beyond concepts. On a more subtle level this dimension of a Buddha is connected to the breath.

The **Mind** of a Buddha is a boundless field of wisdom and compassion, limitless and formless, holding all things with complete openness. There is no longer any sense of separation between self and other but only the spontaneous, effortless play of wisdom manifesting in response to the needs of beings. From this realization, all intentions flow naturally, infused with bodhicitta, the infinite wish for the liberation of all.

Enlightened activity is spontaneous.

- Once realization dawns, there is no hesitation or doubt but only the free and natural expression of wisdom.

- A fully awakened being does not deliberate about how to help others since compassion flows effortlessly.

- There is no fixed method since a Buddha may guide through speech, presence, silence, or direct experience.

This is why enlightened activity is inexhaustible: it is not an effortful striving, but the spontaneous radiance of realization itself.

My teacher Dan Brown used to say "the job description of a Buddha is to express inexhaustible enlightened activity for the benefit of beings." That's a good description.

Like the sun that always shines without trying to bring its light and warmth, the activity of a Buddha never ceases and is effortlessly radiant with light rays of wisdom and love.

## Closing Reflection: The Endless Activity of Enlightenment

Rather than seeking enlightenment as a distant goal, reflect on this:

- What would it mean to act without hesitation, without self-doubt, purely for the benefit of others?

- How would life feel if everything, every emotion, every event, was recognized as an expression of wisdom?

- What if your very existence was already an enlightened display inviting you to deeper compassion.

Once realization dawns, there is nothing to force, nothing to control for it is all spontaneous play. The Three Buddha Bodies stabilize. The Five Wisdom Energies are spontaneously present. All that remains is the endless expression of love and wisdom through the activity of body, speech, and mind.

In the next chapter, we will explore how this awakened activity uniquely expresses itself through five archetypal typologies called the Five Buddha Families.

For now, simply rest in this:

*The Five Wisdom Energies and Three Buddha Bodies are the natural expression of an enlightened mind.*

Chapter 16

# Buddhahood as a Unique Expression

## A Single Realization with a Rainbow of Expressions

In the previous chapter, we explored how enlightenment includes an inexhaustible expression of wisdom and compassion. The Buddha Bodies and the Five Wisdom Energies reveal that enlightenment is an endlessly creative display that meets beings in whatever way they need.

Now, we take this understanding even further. We begin with an inquiry:

Are Buddhas all the same? Or are they unique?

Spoiler alert: They are both!

*All Buddhas have the same Enlightened Awareness, but the expression of that Enlightened Awareness is unique.*

This chapter explores the unique ways in which enlightenment manifests in the world through five archetypal typologies called the five Buddha Families.

In the next few pages, we will explore how the Five Buddha Families represent different enlightened archetypes, each embodying a distinct expression of awakened wisdom. We will see how every Buddha manifests their realization uniquely, revealing enlightenment in a way that is dynamic and personal. Finally, we will examine how you, too, have a natural Buddha family or the unique way in which your own enlightenment will shine.

Enlightenment does not erase uniqueness since it fully reveals it. Just as white light refracts into a rainbow, realization shines through the lens of the unique history, patterns, wisdom energies, and natural inclinations, creating a one-of-a-kind expression of Buddhahood.

## The Five Buddha Families—
## The Archetypes of Enlightenment

Although all Buddhas share the same realization, they do not all express it in the same way. The Five Buddha Families (*panchakula*) represent the five fundamental archetypes of enlightened buddhas or the different ways in which a buddha manifests in the world.

These five buddha families are deeply connected to the Five Wisdom Energies we explored in the previous chapter. However, while the five wisdom energies describe the dynamic qualities of an enlightened mind, the five Buddha families represent distinct archetypal expressions of enlightenment itself. Each Buddha family embodies a unique flavor or type of awakened activity. This typology shapes how wisdom tends to manifest in specific ways in different Buddhas. So, although all buddhas have all five wisdom energies available, the flavor and dominant patterns of expression are different according to the Buddha Family of which they are a part.

Just as pure white light refracts through a prism displaying distinct colors, the very same enlightenment refracts through these five archetypes. Some Buddhas are fierce and unstoppable, others peaceful and radiant with each serving the needs of beings in their own way.

| Buddha Family | How This Type of Buddha Acts in the World | Buddha Archetype | Symbol | Associated Wisdom Energy |
|---|---|---|---|---|
| Vajra | Deeply insightful, cuts through delusion, sharp intellect, precise and penetrating presence | Akshobhya – The Buddha of unwavering clarity, transforming confusion into insight | Dorje | Mirror-like Wisdom |
| Ratna | Generous, nurturing, creates harmony, brings wealth and abundance to others | Ratnasambhava – The Buddha of richness, revealing the preciousness of all beings | Jewel | Wisdom of Equanimity / Sameness |
| Padma | Charismatic, loving, deeply connected to others, draws beings into the Dharma | Amitabha – The Buddha of infinite light, Awakening beings through love and beauty | Lotus | Discriminating Wisdom |
| Karma | Efficient, powerful, skillful, executes great projects for the world | Amoghasiddhi – The Buddha of fearless action, manifesting transformation and accomplishment | Sword | All-Accomplishing Wisdom |
| Buddha | Deeply still, peaceful, vast presence, holds space for all things to arise and pass naturally | Vairocana – The all-encompassing Buddha of vast, spacious awareness | Wheel | Wisdom of the Dharmadhātu |

## The Unique Ways Buddhas Manifest in the World

Each being before enlightenment has a dominant typology, a way that their mind engages the world.

After enlightenment, that same typology does not disappear but it is purified and transformed into an enlightened way of being; a specific kind of Buddha. Understanding your Buddha family enhances your enlightened activity in the world. If we look at the Five Dhyani Buddhas, the original archetypes of each family, we see not one expression of enlightenment, but an clearly differentiated typology:

- **Akshobhya** (**Vajra Family**) – The Buddha of mirror-like wisdom, cutting through delusion with unwavering clarity and transforming anger into insight.

- **Amitabha (Padma Family)** – The Buddha of infinite light and compassion, drawing beings toward enlightenment through love, devotion, and beauty.

- **Amoghasiddhi (Karma Family)** – The Buddha of fearless action, embodying the wisdom of accomplishment and the power to manifest transformation in the world.

- **Ratnasambhava (Ratna Family)** – The Buddha of richness and equanimity, transforming pride into generosity and revealing the sacred preciousness of all beings.

- **Vairocana (Buddha Family)** – The all-encompassing Buddha of vast, spacious awareness, embodying the wisdom of pure, non-dual perception.

When we examine great Buddhas and Bodhisattvas of history and legend, we also see a similar archetypal typology:

- **Manjushri (Vajra Family)** – The embodiment of wisdom, cutting through ignorance like a sword.

- **Kshitigarbha (Karma Family)** – The fearless bodhisattva who vows to liberate beings from the hell realms, demonstrating boundless resolve and action.

- **Samantabhadra (Buddha Family)** – The primordial buddha embodying the dharmadatu itself.

- **Maitreya (Ratna Family)** – The future Buddha, embodying abundance and benevolence, radiating generosity and the promise of an enlightened age.

- **Padmasambhava (Padma Family)** –
  The tantric master who transformed Tibet,
  embodying the magnetizing power of wisdom,
  love, and skillful means.

Each great being expresses the same enlightenment
in their own unique way according to their archetype.

## What Type of Buddha Are You?

Just as each Buddha manifests uniquely, so do you.
You have a unique Buddha family and a particular con-
figuration of wisdom energies.

- Are you precise and sharp, able to see through
  confusion instantly? → You might be a
  representative of the Vajra family.

- Are you naturally abundant, generous, and
  stabilizing? → You might be a representative of
  the Ratna family.

- Do you lead with love, magnetism, and deep
  connection? → You might be a representative of
  the Padma family.

- Do you move with powerful, unstoppable
  action? → You might be a representative of the
  Karma family.

- Do you rest in vast stillness, holding space for
  all things? → You might be a representative of
  the Buddha family.

Stay curious about which archetypal patterns most
resonate with you. This awareness can help enhance
your enlightened activity in the world and keep you alert
to which of the distorted patterns you might be most
susceptible to.

And remember, understanding archetypal patterns
like this is not just another way to reify a solid sense of

self. This is a pattern of manifestation which, once understood, liberates the relative aspects of your being to their highest potential.

You do not need to suppress who you are. Your enlightenment will naturally express itself in its own unique way; without creating identification or obscurations that cloud over your true nature.

So what kind of Buddha are you?

- **A Vajra Buddha** teaches with clarity and insight.

- **A Ratna Buddha** nurtures and creates harmony.

- **A Padma Buddha** draws beings into wisdom with love and connection.

- **A Karma Buddha** gets things done, manifesting great works.

- **A Buddha Buddha** simply is, holding vast space for all things.

There is no one right way to be a Buddha. Enlightenment shines through uniquely, appearing in ways perfectly suited to benefiting others.

## Closing Reflection: Your Unique Buddha Family

Ask yourself these questions:

- Which Buddha family best reflects your natural strengths and patterns?

- If you were already fully awakened, how would your Buddha-Nature express itself in the world?

- What qualities in you, once purified, become a source of benefit for all beings?

- How might your personal path to Awakening

shape the way you naturally guide and inspire others?

• Instead of trying to fit into an ideal of enlightenment, how can you trust the expression of Buddhahood already shining through?

For now, simply remember:

*Your path is unique. Your expression of enlightenment is unique. Let the colors of your unique rainbow shine.*

# Chapter 17

# COMPLETION AND COMPASSION

## The End of the Path, the Beginning of Buddhahood

The path of realization has a destination. It is not endless wandering. The teachings of the gradual path of Lamrim, from the foundations of ethics and concentration to the highest wisdom of Mahamudra and Dzogchen, lead to a definitive realization: the recognition of *Enlightened Awareness*.

In this sense, the path does come to completion. The confusion that once veiled reality dissolves. Suffering ends. The mind that once grasped for something outside itself rests effortlessly in its natural state. This natural state is *originally pure and it knows itself directly and immediately as the true origin of existence itself.*

Yet even with a realization that is complete from the perspective of wisdom, compassionate activity is unceasing.

Buddhism speaks of two truths: the relative and the ultimate.

- **On the ultimate level**, there is nothing to do, nowhere to go, and nothing to attain. Enlightened Awareness is already free and has always been free. When this is realized, the journey ends. This is the way things are.

- **On the relative level,** the world continues.

Suffering still seems to exist. Beings still believe they are caught in illusion. And so, compassion does not end. Compassion is spontaneous and effortless. This is the way things appear.

These two truths are perfectly inseparable. They both share the same supreme root of emptiness.

This is why the greatest masters, even after recognizing Enlightened Awareness, continue to teach, guide, and serve. Not because they need to, not because they are searching for something, but because it is the natural movement of wisdom to express itself to itself as perfect intimacy and compassion.

## Completion

For most, the spiritual path begins with seeking. We feel that something is missing, and we look for answers. We study, meditate, and practice, step by step, refining our understanding.

Then, at some point, we see through the illusion of the whole show. We even see through the idea of the path itself. The path that led us to this very moment is also empty. In this, we recognize what has always been true: that the very awareness reading these words right now is already free, already fully enlightened. This isn't conceptual. It is a direct realization of the primordial nature of Enlightenment. *It's always been this way.*

With this recognition, seeking comes to an end. There is no longer a struggle to "become enlightened" because it's perfectly clear now that enlightenment was never something to attain. Enlightened awareness, with its Buddha Bodies, Wisdom Energies, and archetypal modes of expression, is the way things are and have always been. In this way, Dan Brown used to say that at this level of practice, "You lock into the very structure of reality itself."

## Compassion

The perfection of wisdom naturally gives rise to limitless compassion. Without clinging to a separate self, kindness is no longer effortful. It does not come from obligation or duty but is simply what happens when illusion falls away and all karma is purified.

A fully realized being does not need to think, "I should help others." Instead, they cannot help but help. Compassion is not a practice but is a way of being. Just as the sun's rays are naturally warm, a Buddha's responsiveness is naturally compassionate. And skillful means can be refined infinitely.

From the perspective of an ordinary being it may look like a Buddha performs selfless service. But from the perspective of an enlightened being there is only the natural flow of primordial wisdom spontaneously expressing itself to itself.

A single full moon is reflected in many buckets of water that are placed on the ground. The single moon appears as many. Likewise, a single buddha is reflected in many minds of perceiving beings. It appears as if buddha-like copies have been made that are perfectly suited to meet the precise needs of each and every being.

Bringing completion and compassion into a single gesture, the Great Dzogchen Master, Nyoshul Khen Rinpoche, has a remarkable way of putting it. He says:

*Suffering has no beginning but it has an end. Enlightenment has a specific beginning but it has no end.*

Suffering comes to an end. Enlightened activity does not. Buddhahood is a dynamic, ever-blossoming expression of reality itself, uniquely tailored to this moment, and this moment, and this moment…

If you take any wisdom from this book, let it be this:

- **Realization is possible.** Enlightenment is not reserved for the few but is possible for you. Just start walking the path.

- **You do not need to endlessly seek.** The path does have an end. You can complete the path in this very life.

- **Even when the path of wisdom is complete, love and spontaneous compassionate activity never cease.**

This is the meaning of completion and compassion.

Just before he passed from his physical body, while I was kneeling at his bedside, Dan asked me to share something very specific with any students I interacted with in the future. It was one of his final requests. In a quiet but crystal clear whisper, he said: "Make sure students know it doesn't take a long time."

Please take a moment to let the magnitude of that statement sink in: *Enlightenment doesn't take a long time.*

Buddhahood is your true nature. *There are no prerequisites.* Recognizing your own enlightened mind doesn't happen in time. It is simply the way things already are. Don't let time stand in the way, especially as you explore this gradual path. Enlightenment doesn't take a long time.

*A buddha is fully free and fully feeling.* A buddha is wide open like space and yet perfectly intimate with all form. A buddha spontaneously and effortlessly illuminates the path to enlightenment.

In this way, and in every way, a buddha is a true *lamp of wisdom.*

*May there always be enlightened teachers.*
*May there always be teachings.*
*May all beings come to recognize their own essence as Enlightened Awareness. May Everything Good Flourish!*

# A

- **All-Accomplishing Wisdom** – The enlightened ability to act effortlessly and spontaneously for the benefit of all beings, transforming restlessness and manipulation into skillful enlightened action.

- **Attachment** – The grasping or clinging to experiences, objects, or relationships, which leads to suffering.

- **Awakened Awareness** – The recognition of one's true nature as lucid, boundless, centerless awareness.

# B

- **Bodhicitta** – The awakened heart-mind, the aspiration and commitment to attain enlightenment for the benefit of all beings.

- **Buddha Families** – Five archetypal expressions of enlightenment, each associated with a particular wisdom energy and transformed emotion.

- **Buddha-Nature** – The inherent potential for enlightenment present within all beings.

# C

- **Compassion** – The wish for all beings to be free from suffering, expressed through skillful and loving action.

- **Conditional Giving** – A near enemy of generosity, where one gives with expectations of return or recognition.

- **Cruelty** – The far enemy of compassion, manifesting as indifference or harm toward others.

-

# D

- **Dharma** – The teachings of the Buddha and the path of truth leading to liberation.

- **Dharmadhātu Wisdom** – The wisdom of vast openness, revealing all phenomena as naturally perfect and empty of inherent existence.

- **Dharmakāya** – One of the three bodies of a buddha. This is the formless, ultimate reality of a Buddha, beyond all conceptual elaboration.

- **Depersonalization** – A negative psychological state in which one feels detached from their own thoughts, emotions, or body, often arising in deep meditation as the result of trauma.

- **Derealization** – A negative sense of detachment from the external world, where reality appears distant or unreal.

- **Discriminating Wisdom:** The wisdom of perfect intimacy and precise discernment, directly perceiving the uniqueness of each experience while remaining free from attachment.

- **Dissociation** – A negative psychological state that feels disconnected from experience, often arising as a defense mechanism.

# E

- **Ego-Clinging** – The habitual tendency to identify with and grasp onto a fixed sense of self.

- **Emptiness (Shunyata)** – The insight that all phenomena are devoid of inherent existence and arise dependently.

- **Envy** – The far enemy of Sympathetic Joy, manifesting as resentment or longing for what others have.

• **Equanimity** – A balanced, unbiased mind that remains open, accepting, and non-reactive toward all experiences and beings.

• **Equanimity Wisdom** – The wisdom of even-mindedness and sameness that perceives all beings as equal in their essence. This wisdom reveals the inherent dignity and preciousness of every being.

# F

• **False Refuge** – Seeking security in impermanent or external things instead of true refuge in the awakened nature.

• **Five Buddha Families** – The five different archetypal expressions of Enlightened Awareness.

• **Four Immeasurables** – The four boundless qualities: equanimity, unconditional love, compassion, and sympathetic joy.

• **Four Yogas of Mahamudrā** – The progressive stages of realization in Mahamudrā practice: One-Pointedness (stabilizing attention), Non-Elaboration (seeing emptiness directly), One Taste (recognizing all phenomena as inseparable from awareness), and Non-Meditation (effortlessness and the recognition of Awakened Awareness).

# G

• **Generosity (Dana)** – The first of the Six Perfections, embodying selfless giving without attachment or expectation of gain.

• **Greed** – The far enemy of generosity, manifesting as selfish desire and hoarding.

• **Guru Yoga** – A devotional practice that invokes the presence of the teacher to merge with their awakened wisdom.

# H

• **Habitual Patterns** – Deeply ingrained tendencies that condition perception and behavior, often leading to suffering.

• **Hatred** – The far enemy of unconditional love, manifesting as hostility or aversion.

# I

• **Ignorance** – A fundamental misunderstanding of reality, obscuring the recognition of one's true nature.

• **Impermanence** – The truth that all phenomena, including thoughts and emotions, are constantly changing.

• **Indifference** – A near enemy of equanimity, where one disengages emotionally rather than remaining open, present, and fully feeling.

• **Insight Meditation (Vipashyana)** – A practice of directly seeing the nature of mind and phenomena.

• **Interdependent Origination** – The principle that all things arise in dependence on causes and conditions.

# J

• **Jealousy** – A negative mental state which fears the loss of something one already possesses. This is transformed into All-Accomplishing Wisdom.

# K

• **Karma** – The law of cause and effect, shaping experiences based on past actions.

• **Karmic Obscurations** – The habitual tendencies and mental imprints that veil clear awareness and pure vision.

• **Kāya** – A term referring to the different "bodies" of a Buddha's enlightened presence.

# L

- **Lama (Soul Mother):** A spiritual guide who nurtures and awakens the disciple's realization.

# M

- **Madhyamaka (Middle Way Philosophy)** – The philosophical school emphasizing emptiness and the absence of inherent existence.

- **Mahamudrā** – A profound system of meditation revealing the nature of mind. This system includes the Four Yogas.

- **Meditation (Dhyana)** – The practice of cultivating stability, clarity, and insight.

- **Mirror-Like Wisdom** – The wisdom that reflects reality exactly as it is, free from distortion.

# N

- **Near Enemies** – Subtle distortions of virtues that appear similar but lack their depth (e.g., pity as a near enemy of compassion).

- **Nirmanakaya** – The physical manifestation of a Buddha in the world as a display of compassion.

- **Nonduality** – The realization that subject and object, self and other, are not separate.

- **Non-Meditation** – A stage of practice where awareness is naturally present without effort.

# O

- **Ordinary Deluded Mind** – The default, reactive state of consciousness before insight and realization.

# P

- **Padma Energy** – The wisdom energy associated with passion, love, and magnetism.

- **Patience (Kshanti)** – Meeting difficulties with stability and compassion.

- **Pity** – The near enemy of compassion, arising as a sense of superiority or condescension toward those who suffer, rather than genuine empathy and connection.

- **Precious Human Birth** – The rare and fortunate opportunity of being born with the capacity to attain enlightenment.

# R

- **Ratna Energy** – The wisdom energy associated with generosity, preciousness, and stability.

- **Reactivity** – The habitual tendency to react impulsively rather than responding with awareness.

- **Refuge** – Taking shelter in the Three Jewels: the Buddha, Dharma, and Sangha.

- **Rigpa** – The direct recognition of one's innate, awakened awareness.

# S

- **Sambhogakāya** – The body of enjoyment where Buddhas experience pure vision and a sacred world.

- **Samādhi** – Deep meditative absorption.

- **Samsāra** – The cycle of conditioned existence characterized by suffering.

- **Sangha** – The community of practitioners supporting one another on the path.

- **Six Perfections** – Generosity, ethical conduct, patience, joyful effort, meditation, and wisdom.

- **Sympathetic Joy (Mudita)** – The heartfelt delight in the happiness and success of others, free from self-interest.

# T

- **Three Poisons** – The root delusions of attachment, aversion, and ignorance.

- **Trikaya (Three Buddha Bodies):** The threefold nature of a Buddha's enlightened expression— Dharmakaya (formless truth body), Sambhogakaya (radiant bliss body), and Nirmanakaya (manifested embodiment).

# V

- **Vajra Energy** – The wisdom energy associated with clarity, precision, and insight.

- **Vipaśyanā – Insight Meditation:** The practice of seeing clearly or seeing through (Tib. *lak-tong*), cultivating direct insight into impermanence, emptiness, and the mind's true nature beyond conceptualization.